T0196976

THE
HARDEST
PATH

A Journey Outside to Answer the Questions Within

Matt Jardine

BALBOA
PRESS

A DIVISION OF HAY HOUSE

Balboa Press books may be ordered through booksellers or by contacting:

Balboa Press
A Division of Hay House
1663 Liberty Drive
Bloomington, IN 47403
www.balboapress.com
1 (877) 407-4847

Print information available on the last page.

ISBN: 978-1-5043-7206-0 (sc)
ISBN: 978-1-5043-7207-7 (hc)
ISBN: 978-1-5043-7220-6 (e)

Library of Congress Control Number: 2016921016

Balboa Press rev. date: 12/20/2016

CONTENTS

I think it is best to create stories of your own
Until then you are very welcome to mine.

FOREWORD

As a martial artist and former professional fighter, I live by the philosophy of *Yamato-damashii* – the Samurai Spirit or the Unbreakable Spirit. Even after my retirement, I am always in search of ways to build my spirit and to find the means to cultivate my soul to become a better man.

I took an interest in the Shikoku 88 temple pilgrimage because I saw it as a way to test myself. Making this 880-mile pilgrimage, I knew I would experience types of trials and hardships that I've never faced in my forty-eight years of existence here on earth.

The Shikoku pilgrimage is a journey of self-discovery as well as a challenge to push yourself to your physical, mental, and emotional limits day after day. It is a gruelling trek, and when the pilgrim completes it, he will have a very different way of viewing life. The pilgrim learns to push himself to his limits, and the pilgrimage teaches him to appreciate many simple things in life that most overlook or take for granted.

I have a new outlook on life, and I am much more at peace with myself, something I could not have attained otherwise.

Enson Inoue
Former Shooto Heavyweight Champion

Top: Goshuin of Ryōzenji, Temple 1

Middle: The Hannya Shingyō, hand calligraphed by Hajime-san

Bottom: Goshuin of Ōkuboji, Temple 88

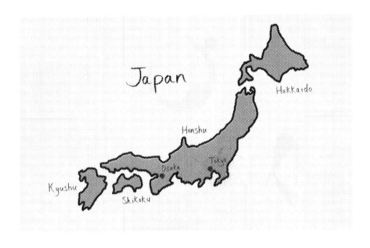

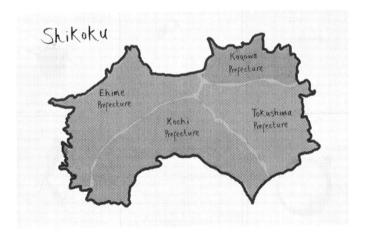

INTRODUCTION

Seek not to walk in the footsteps of the Masters,
Seek what they sought.

—Journal entry

I never read the instructions that come with flat pack furniture. I prefer to dive in headfirst. Over the years my wife has learnt to stay quiet as she watches me undo the mistakes I could have avoided by reading the instructions that come with flat pack furniture. This time, though, she gave me a look and advice that even I couldn't ignore. "At the very least," she told me, "you will have to explain a little about the idea of pilgrimage. Not everyone gets it," she warned, "and you'll have to explain your obsession with Japan too." So here it is. I bow to higher forces; always it seems, but I still won't read flat pack instructions, no matter how hard my wife glares at me.

Pilgrimage: it's tricky trying to explain something that you think you fully understand but can't quite seem to articulate to those who say that they don't. My son, now mid-GCSEs, often asks me the meaning of words during his English homework, "You don't know, do you, Dad?" putting his arm around my shoulder and squeezing tight with his bench press–developed lats and pecs. I fit snugly inside his chest these days. If his squeeze gets any stronger, I will have to find a way to stop his burgeoning power before he challenges for the alpha male role in our household. I may have to do it while he's sleeping or not looking.

"Actually, smarty pants, I do. I just can't quite fully explain it. I do know, but …." I realise it's not a great answer for a writer. After all, it is our job to describe experiences to the uninitiated. But I think the difficulty in trying to explain the concept of pilgrimage is far more justified; it is an ethereal topic that eludes the confines of dictionary exactitude. One dictionary attempts to describe pilgrimage as: "a journey to a sacred place or shrine". Having walked one, I would like to expand on this a little: "Pilgrimage is a long, tiring and often monotonous walk to a sacred place or shrine".

How did *sacred*, *holy*, and *religious* come to be synonymous with struggle and pain? When did self-flagellation become a noble deed? The concept of subjecting ourselves to turmoil to reach enlightened states of happiness seems crazy to me, a perverse joke by those in charge of this thing they call living, whoever they may be. Yet people have chosen pilgrimage as a method of self-reflecting hardship for generations. I reckon it sits with the top five most punishing routes to peace. It has helped countless devotees find answers to their own pressing questions of life: Why are we here? Is there more to life than this? What happens after we die? Why can't I find love? Why can I always find love, but with crazy people? Why do I never have enough money? How can I get to the Bahamas with the change I've found down the back of the sofa? These are merely a snapshot of a pilgrim's musings.

Before writing and selling sixty-five million copies of *The Alchemist*, Brazilian maestro Paulo Coelho wrote *The Pilgrimage*. It was about his walk of the Camino de Santiago, a European pilgrimage coursing through France to the shrine of St James the Great in Galicia, north-western Spain. It is one part adventure story, one part guide to self-discovery. After reading it, I decided that I too would walk a pilgrimage.

There are two types of decisions made in life: "I'd like to do that" and "I'm going to do that". The first comes with a vague, dull, and subtly nauseating sensation that sits heavy in the gut and groans its disbelief at us: "Really? OK. Whatever …." The second is an altogether different prospect. In the moment of our declaration, lightning shards of commitment pierce clouds of doubt. A seraphic song sings to our heart, "Thy will be done, my child, thy will be done", and our step becomes light as though we were now wearing Hermes' super sneakers. We are encouraged to press on towards our goal without further ado. Or something like that.

My decision to walk a pilgrimage was a "gonna" rather than a "liketa". The Camino de Santiago didn't appeal. Memories of childhood holidays on the Costa del Brit robbed me of an affinity for walking the Camino. I didn't like the idea of traipsing the trail wearing a knotted hanky to ward off the midday sun and humming football chants to ease my troubled soul. True or not, the vision would not budge. I decided that my journey must be to a country that has always inspired me (my wife calls it an obsession), a country that it is short of neither spiritual trails, holy endeavour, nor craziness: Japan.

Japan and "the 88": I have had an inexplicable fascination with Japan for as long as I can remember. I have no idea why. I'd never been there, my parents had never been, and I didn't know anyone who had ever been. It's much the same phenomenon as thumbing through a brochure and being drawn to some countries and not to others. When my wife and I travel, we like to compare our gut instincts about a place and our relationship to it. Some places feel like home to us, others we are ambivalent about, and yet others still are repellent to us. I wonder if maybe we lived there in a former life. She stops listening to me and goes in search of a baggage trolley and bureau de change when I start talking like this.

When I was eleven, my parents fanned the flames of my Japanese love affair and did something that shot my passion into the stratosphere – something I have never forgotten. One of two great feelings in life is being awakened and told that you aren't going to school on a school day. The other is when you discover that you aren't going to school on a school day, but your brother is. (It still lifts my heart thirty years later.) Instead, my parents would be taking me to visit London's Victoria and Albert Museum for an exhibition of the samurai – the aristocracy and warrior class of Japan.

The cold steel and unique curves of the famous Japanese sword, warrior helmets sculpted in the image of protective deities, suits of armour engineered with detail ahead of its time, the crisp black of inked *kanji* (the ideograms of Japan's language) filling the white space of imperial scrolls – who wouldn't be inspired and find their adult life tilted toward learning more about this exotic culture? Years later then, it was only natural, or fateful, that the two would marry: pilgrimage and Japan.

In Japan, they call it the *hachi jū hachi,* the 88 temple pilgrimage. It is their most venerated holy route. The number 88 represents the 88 sacred temples that constitute the pilgrimage. You must visit each temple for the journey to be complete. Scattered temples course a circumference of Shikoku, one of the four islands that constitute Japan's mainland; the other three are Kyushu, Honshu, and Hokkaido. The journey is circular rather than linear, as are many of its European counterparts, an important difference that demonstrates a fundamental contrast between Western and Eastern philosophy.

Often, in the West, life is viewed as a climb; scaling the corporate ladder, moving up the grades from reception to university, aspiring upwards towards heaven at the end of life. The East adopts a more cyclical model. A belief in rebirth allows the view of continuation. Never-ending upward spirals, if you live positively, never-ending downward spirals, if your life choices have been unkind. This endless cycle of birth, death, and rebirth, transcended only by enlightenment, is the holy grail of many Eastern religions, spiritual systems, and philosophies. Walking the 88 is considered one such method of attaining this exalted state. It is no coincidence then that the *hachi jū hachi* has 88 temples. Turn this number on its side and it is the symbol of eternity and cyclical continuation – a reminder of what it is the pilgrim is hoping to transcend.

Walking it feels like an eternity: 1,400 kilometres of gruelling terrain, flats, and farmlands, mountains and hills, bamboo groves and copses, concrete jungles and soulless cities, temples and sacred sites. It is heaven and earth in one journey. All of the thoughts, emotion, and circumstance that constitute the rich macrocosm of a full and lengthy life are experienced in microcosm while on pilgrimage, as with the mayfly that lives its entire life from birth to maturation and death in the space of a single day. Undistracted by the usual routine, we can concentrate on our attitudes to this life lived in concentrate. These insights alone can be enlightening, if not in the religious sense.

If walking, the advice is to allow at least forty to fifty days.

Nowadays, tourists bus around it in a weekend, "selfies" at each temple proving to friends and family that they "did the *hachi jū hachi*", another box to tick on a lifetime of to-dos. But these modern methods fail to plumb the depths of a gruelling, self-reflecting journey.

Life lessons, it seems, are revealed only to faithful pilgrims, not to tourists. Not as some gift from a God on high for penance paid while in hiking shoes, but because lessons only show themselves amidst energy spent and experience collected. Visiting St Paul's on a day trip, for example, would not be the same as arriving with the sole purpose of praying for the returning health of a friend. How can it be any other way?

Pilgrimage is more than starting and finishing. It is an overused but nevertheless correct cliché that the journey is more important than the destination. To whiz around the 88 on a coach is to miss the power, the wonder, and the lessons of living the journey as monks of old: walk the whole way, offer prayers at each temple, sleep where sleep takes you, and learn what you learn. I was always going to walk the *hachi jū hachi* in this manner, in the ways of past traditional spiritual seekers. It was doing it this way, the way of old, that made it life-changing; and it was life-changing because it was so wonderfully life-affirming.

In the town of Hiwasa stands Yakuōji, Temple 23. From the balcony of its single-storey pagoda you look out across the Pacific Ocean from where every year, between May and August, sea turtles arrive to lay their eggs. I had eaten very little for the last three days on the road and had managed to save enough pocket change to pay for a night's rest in the town's YMCA. I stood alone inside the reception area staring across to a wall daubed with the most intense artwork I had ever seen. The artist had used thick reds and blacks in the calligraphy style of Sumi-e, the beautiful art of Japanese ink painting. The form was not traditional; it had an arty, modern, and strangely occult feel to it. I admired it, but it unsettled me as I untied and took off my walking shoes.

"You like?" came a sudden voice at my shoulder that startled me into a pounding heart and slightly squeaky voice. From where in the shadows had this guy appeared? He was the YMCA manager. A tubby little Japanese in a 1980s-style shell suit and of indeterminate age, as many Japanese are. He told me a few important things:

1. What time I had to check out.
2. That I would need to kick the door of the washing machine, gently, on closing before it would whir into action.
3. That I was the rebirth of Kōbō Daishi (the founding saint of the 88 temple pilgrimage) and that I was to complete the whole journey on foot despite any and all hardship I would encounter. I was then to share all that had I learned with the rest of the world, for the happiness and betterment of all.

Erm, all right then, I was just looking for a room for the night ....

CHAPTER 1

Sage and Wisdom Pie –
A Winning Recipe

If you knew you could have anything,
What would you wish for?
—*Journal entry*

CHINESE SAGE LAO TZU is quoted as teaching that "a journey of a thousand miles begins with a single step". The hell it does! I don't mean to cast aspersions on Lao Tzu's abilities to teach, but he only had half the story. A journey of a thousand miles actually begins with the *decision* to start one of a thousand miles – or four or ten or however many you choose to travel.

Julio Iglesias said much the same when he sang "Begin the Beguine" in his sexy Spanish lilt to drooling crowds of infatuated women back in the 1980s. Julio wasn't quite saying the same as Lao Tzu, but nevertheless, I use his example for a couple of reasons. Every Sunday afternoon throughout my childhood, "Begin the Beguine" blared out from my parents' hi-fi system. I'm sure I heard him singing "Begin the Begin". At least that's the line that stayed with me ever since, and that's the line I suddenly find myself singing from time to time in the most random places at the most random times: at traffic lights, buying cheese, stretching, writing. And "begin the begin" perfectly describes that moment of decision-making that precedes the start of anything.

The other reason for my preference of Julio over Lao Tzu is that I detest Western social media's rape of genuine Far Eastern wisdom and

1

meaning, with its overuse of feel-good memes, T-shirt slogans, and bumper stickers. That noise you hear is Lao turning uncomfortably in his grave. Don't get me wrong, I love Eastern wisdom: Chinese, Japanese, Korean, Vietnamese, Indian, Tibetan – you name it, I love it. I have spent my life around both the Eastern martial arts and Far Eastern healing therapies. The martial arts I teach to this day; the healing I use as my primary go-to if I'm feeling under the weather. My issue is with the pseudo-sages of the West, those who proliferate martial arts schools, yoga clubs, and alternative therapy courses up and down the country.

I was told many times, by non-Japanese martial arts teachers, that to visit a traditional Japanese *dōjō* in Japan was a very complicated affair wrought with almost unassailable complexity. "It's because of their culture and complexities of etiquette", they told me. I remember my teacher having a far-off look as he said it that made me look behind me to see where on earth he was staring. I would need a "special introduction" from him. He was my gateway to the traditional Eastern arts. When I was "ready", he would "fix it", he told me. Wow. Thank you, Master. Years later, I was still practicing my karate in a Twickenham church hall and not in Japan. The closest I had come to training with real Japanese was when Kato joined for a week and then left. He preferred the judo club down the road in Molesey.

Eventually, despite my teacher's insistence that he would choose the time of my Japanese travels, I decided to go with or without the elusive formal introduction. Once there, I was prepared to take the risk of being beaten savagely for my impertinence, but I figured it was worth a try. I was beginning to wonder if my teacher had been stalling my journey to the East. I pondered if maybe I was a student not worthy of an invite, or if he was a teacher without credentials to secure one.

My plane touched down in Okinawa, the Japanese island where the art of karate had been created centuries before. In martial arts terms, I was home. With just my karate uniform and two belts, a black one and a white one, I found my way to the dojo of arguably the most famous karate teacher of our time, Master Morio Higaonna. More than a little nervous, and acutely aware that I was without formal introduction, I slid open the door to the main training hall. The thought played heavily on my mind, my shirt now wet with more than just the clinging damp of Okinawan humidity.

I entered with merely the manners parents teach any child when arriving at someone else's home: wipe your feet, smile, don't be a putz. Master Higaonna greeted me with the widest smile. His hands callused from years of hitting stone, wood, and people, he tapped me warmly on the back and invited me in to join the class. I offered to wear the white belt of a beginner in place of my black belt, in recognition that I was nothing in his world (I had read on the Internet that this was a good thing to do). "Why?" he asked with a puzzled look. "Aren't you proud of your black belt?"

"Yes, *Shihan*, very proud."

"Then put it on, Mattō-san; we all just do karate here. Welcome." And that was that. The beginning of insights into what my *shiatsu* teacher used to call "strange English ways".

Shiatsu, as I used to explain to new patients to my London-based treatment room, is acupuncture without the needles. Most of them had heard of acupuncture at least, so I almost always used it as a reference. Japanese in origin, shiatsu is a highly effective form of alternative/complementary bodywork therapy using pressure points, massage, stretching, and other techniques to help restore, rejuvenate, or just plain relax the recipient. Martial arts students often learn it so that they can heal the damage they may potentially deliver as karate opponents. Killing your training partners leads to lonely times in the dojo, some soon realized. The yin balancing the yang, to use traditional Eastern Asian medical parlance, seemed a logical solution.

Mr Ohashi was a little Japanese shiatsu master and teacher with a jet-black pudding-bowl haircut, a radiant smile, and the thickest jam-jar glasses you have ever seen. His accent was so obvious, it sounded more like a parody than a genuine one. If you can picture Edna "E" Mode from Disney's *The Incredibles*, you have Mr Ohashi—just change the accent. "Mattō-san, you English are very strange," he once told me. "You love Japan. That is very good, but you are not Japanese. You should not try to be Japanese. I do not try to be English." Ohashi told me that, from his experience of teaching seminars in the UK, if he taught only in Japanese, using an English translator, he would have more students attend his lectures than if he taught in English. And his English was impeccable.

But why do these strange phenomena exist? It seems we are simply in love with the romance of the East. We like the idea of a far-off land that emerges from the mist where bald-headed masters fight, pray, and love. They are lands far enough away, with language and culture so alien to our own, that we can easily believe our imaginings without the troublesome problem of truth shattering them.

If the worst that happened with these false notions was merely deluded misrepresentation, then I wouldn't have to sit so squarely in the saddle of my proverbial high horse. But the truth is that such romantic ideas of Eastern martial arts could lead to a false sense of physical confidence regarding self-defence, while the same attitude to Eastern therapies could lead to a dangerous reliance on remedies that, on the whole, are not comprehensively proven in the treatment of life-threatening illness. It is probably best to fight cancer with radiation, not reiki.

Of course, once the romantics have bombarded us with tie-dyed yoga trousers and long, wispy grey beards and spoken to us in that sickly sweet tone of the passive-aggressive for long enough, then the realists shut down and become resistant to any of the genuine wisdom that proliferates from the East. "You had me at hello", said Dorothy to title character Jerry Maguire. "You lost me at lavender and chakra," said everyone else to the Western hippie lovers of Eastern culture.

Great wisdom and magic come from the East. Of that you can be sure. But back to Julio and the first lesson learned from the 88 temple pilgrimage, a lesson taught not in Japan but back in Surrey before even arriving. Before you can begin anything, you must first decide to do so. ("Begin the Beguine" – there is Iglesias again in my head, the Spanish earworm.) I suggest that deciding to start anything is the single most underestimated skill in the universe. Arriving at a place of firm decision involves difficult terrain, a pilgrimage in itself.

The major obstacles are uncertainty, fear, and doubt. To make a decision, first you must know what you want. Years as children typically being told to "put it down", "You can't have that today", "Money doesn't grow on trees", and "Stop daydreaming" have taken away our confidence in decision-making regarding our innate desires. We look towards others for rules, direction, and approval. Our wants are mostly their wants, if we are honest with ourselves.

It is important to remember how to dream, as we once did, before deciding which dreams we would love to turn into reality. Which of them are just vague interests, and which pique our attention? Which ones light up our instincts and scream delight at us? Our dreams are pleading to be noticed from under the weight of our suppression and repression.

Here then, is a little technique I was once taught to help us discover our innermost passions.

First, jot down the things that come to mind when you ask yourself the following questions: What would I do with my life if money were absolutely no object, barrier, or boundary? What would I do? What would I have? Who would I be?

Second (be sure not to edit your thoughts too much), note your answers to this: What would I do, be, and have in my life if I had six totally pain- and stress-free months to live?

And finally: What would I do, what would I have, and who would I be when faced with both of the above: endless money but only six months to use it?

I was told that the answers that first come to us after we delve into the questions are our deepest passions. Go after them.

But I hear you protest, despite the dreaming, I don't have all the money in the world, nor the time either. I said the very same thing when I first learnt this technique. Therein lies the problem.

CHAPTER 2

Don't Be a Proper Charlie

Explaining the hachi jū hachi to a soul who has never walked,
Is like trying to explain flying to a soul who has never flown.
—Journal entry

TIME AND MONEY have been cited as obstacles to human endeavour for as long as humans have had endeavour – the call from within to chase our dreams dampened by reminders of economics, schedules, routines, and responsibility.

Stand amongst parents in any school playground at either picking up or dropping off time, and listen to the silent cacophony: the white noise of unvoiced complaint furrowed across brows and expressed in body language, in protest against lives lived unfulfilled. "If only there were enough time and money", whisper tired eyes, "then the life of our dreams would be ours", they suppose.

We all love our families, of course, but the longing to be more still permeates, despite our commitment to them. The guilt of striving doesn't quite manage to silence our instinct's digs that there is more to life than the endless rounds on this giant hamster wheel of daily chore.

Have you ever felt that you are a part of something bigger, grander, and more meaningful than the day-to-day grind? Words are not enough to describe it, this bigness. Do they even exist for something we can neither see nor touch but instinctively know must be there?

I remember my first shoulder rub with this nameless thing. I was around ten years old, I think. The problem with my memory is that it likes to pigeonhole everything but the immediate into a nostalgic time when I was ten, growing up in our family home. This nameless rub could have been any time, but I think I was ten. The three klonks on the dining room ceiling from my mum's broom handle muffled through the bath water where I lay submerged, eyes closed and toasty warm. It didn't startle me, I was far too sleepy for that, but it did let me know that I needed to get out now and come down for dinner.

I stood drip-drying, draped in two towels, in front of the antique mirror that Nan used to own which now filled the whole of the bathroom wall in our house. Mum always told me off for using more towels than I needed ("You don't need two, you little thing") and for leaving them on the bathroom floor for her to pick up. I still do both, except she doesn't pick them up anymore. Nor does my wife. I do. Eventually.

The mirror was completely steamed up with only my outline visible behind it. Usually I would draw pictures in the condensation. Mum used to tell me off for that as well ("Keep your mucky paws off of my mirrors and windows, Matthew Jardine"). I still do it when I go down to visit them in Cornwall. It is childish behaviour, and she still uses my full name when telling me off.

It was then, as I stood drying and chewing the edge of my towel, when I got both a feeling and an image of a flame glowing right at my centre. I don't know where I mean by "my centre". It just seemed to be somewhere right in my middle. I couldn't see it for real; the image was just a certainty in my mind's eye. I could see it no more clearly by looking more closely than you can see a sparrow hawk that crosses your periphery on a country walk. It didn't seem strange, or frightening or particularly poignant. It just felt right, and I was certain about it. As time went on, I began to sense that the same flame that glowed at my middle burned brightly at the centre of all other things too. The connection between both made me feel part of both: me and all other things, alive and together.

In contrast, death and abandonment scared the wits out of me as a child. The thought of it would make me tear around the house trying to escape the grim thoughts threatening to terrorise me by arising inside my head. My parents would often have to intercept my sprints and hold me close in their arms until the terror subsided and I passed out, asleep, in their clutch. Sometimes, perversely, I would make myself think about death, to a point just short of hysteria. I could keep myself just on the right side of terror mostly, sometimes not. I would have to sprint around the house again at those times.

Rare is the person who has never wondered at, or had an experience of, the thing that sits at the very heart and start of life. Religion has made its life work to name and proselytise it; science to prove or disprove it; philosophy to boggle minds about it. Yet we all must consider it, at one time or another, if only because the reality of death forces us to search eventually for a meaning to life and to wonder at what, if anything, transcends it. Time, money, life after death, the meaning of life – these and many others are the questions that pilgrims also ponder.

"Where did you say you were going?" asked my playground parent buddy, Charlie, as he waved his Alfie into class.

"Shikoku-Japan," I answered doing the same to my son.

"Why?"

"To walk the *hachi jū hachi*, Japan's super pilgrimage," I told him.

"Oh." I could see and hear his brain cogs whirring, trying to process and formulate an opinion about it. "Why?" Words found, Charlie started again.

"Oh I don't know, Charlie; challenge myself, think about life a bit, because I just want to," I said.

Charlie apparently did not approve. A life living by the books had helped him master a wordless and disapproving body language. He didn't like anything even slightly off kilter. My dad is a Londoner from the East End, and I grew up around Cockney rhyming slang; Charlie was indeed a right proper one.

A disapproving guilt-laden stance has the power to drive us back into the shadows if we let it. It was a standard tactic for our parents' and grandparents' generation, post–Second World War, in a time not yet accustomed to the new opportunity. I remember my nan using it on me all the time. She did love a piece of good old-fashioned guilt.

"So who is going to look after your two then, while you are

gallivanting around Japan?" he poked, referring to the care of my two young children.

"They've got a mother, Charlie," I poked back. "I think they can all survive for a month without me."

Charlie changed tack; he'd get to me somehow. "You know, as a self-employed business owner, you won't earn while you're away. Can you afford the trip and the time away? Can your family afford it?"

"No, Charlie, not really."

"And all this 'thinking about life' nonsense, what's that all about?" I saw him smirk a little; he was on a roll.

"Charlie, don't you ever wonder if there's more to life? More than all this?"

"Nothing is more important to me than my Alfie," he concluded.

Apparently, that was that. No more to be said. Charlie had spoken.

Charlie was not the first resistance I had faced with my decision to walk the 88. And he certainly wouldn't be the last. That's the funny thing with people. Many don't like to see you trying to better yourself, enjoy yourself or push on. That's the reason many of us abort our dreams, desires, and grand plans. But this resistance didn't matter actually, because even before walking a single step of the pilgrimage, I had already learnt its most valuable lesson: that a whole-hearted decision, founded on passion, had started a ball rolling that would now be impossible to stop.

Under my bed, written in a red hardback original that smells the way only antique books can, are the most beautiful words regarding this very subject. W. H. Murray, from his book *The Scottish Himalayan Expedition*, confirms to us the magic that emanates from a committed decision:

> Until one is committed, there is hesitancy, the chance to draw back, always ineffectiveness. Concerning all acts of initiative (and creation), there is one elementary truth, the ignorance of which kills countless ideas and splendid plans: that the moment one definitely commits oneself, then Providence moves too. All

sorts of things occur to help one that would never otherwise have occurred. A whole stream of events issues from the decision, raising in one's favour all manner of unforeseen incidents and meetings and material assistance, which no man could have dreamt would have come his way.

Perfect.

It was true of expeditions to the Himalayas, of a pilgrimage in Japan, and of any decision that may be made by anyone, anywhere, doing anything. Not even a right proper Charlie could stop me. Of that, I was certain.

CHAPTER 3

Angels at Check-In

Beautiful people everywhere,
But do you have time to hear their songs?
—Journal entry

Formula One superstar Jenson Button was ahead of me in the queue at the airport when I arrived at check-in for my flight to Osaka, Japan. It took the doe-eyed girl behind the counter a few moments to recover from her brief time with the handsome devil (damn him) and inform me that I was "nice and early, but at the wrong airport – this is Heathrow, not Gatwick, sir."

My best friend is Italian. We have a love–hate relationship. Since I've known Alessandro, I've enjoyed verbally abusing him for all his archetypical Italian shortcomings. He uses twelve words when one will do, gesticulating himself into a frenzy. While keeping one hand permanently on the horn, he will attempt to drive a car into space only big enough for a moped, and he always, always arrives anywhere, with only heart attack–ridden minutes left to spare. He laughs at me and tells me to take my punctual, organised, repressed Victorian finger out of my backside. I show him the British "V".

My first thought, then, on being told I was at the wrong airport was *I have to make sure Alessandro never finds out about this; I'll never hear the bloody last of it.* My second thought was, that this was not the most auspicious start to my pilgrimage. W. H. Murray never said anything about this sort of unforeseen circumstance. Where the hell was

Providence now? Were the heavens conspiring to stop my reverential endeavours before they literally got off the ground? Was this trip simply not meant to be? Did I even subscribe to a theory of fate? My heart sank, and my stomach knotted a little; the familiar heat of bubbling frustration reddening my skin, an unpleasant blend of fluctuating fear and anger.

"Sir", the girl behind the counter interrupted my swirling thoughts, "I think someone may be looking out for you up there." She pointed skyward. "We have found one seat available on the next flight from here. You will arrive in Osaka a little earlier than your Gatwick flight. My manager said you could have it; we'll hold it for you."

"Oh", I managed, jolted out of my growing panic and feeling now somewhat guilty for doubting the heavens', and Murray's, ability to deliver the goods. "Thank you." As I headed off to the departure gates, I had to chuckle at my change in fortunes - and the pendulum of my attitude. From distrust in fate in one moment, to a firm belief in life's helping hand in the next. How fickle our faiths, how fluctuating our spiritual determination.

Just a quick note to the powers that be: If you gave us more proof of your existence, it would be easier to believe. If you gave us exactly what we want when we ask for it, it would be simpler to have faith. If you leave aside symbolism and just show us what you can do, we would follow you to the ends of the earth. Probably. – Hello, are you listening?

Buoyed by my good fortune and now with some spare time in hand, I breezed through passport control feeling light and hopeful and into one of the many restaurants that populate airports. Boarding called and meal finished, I gave my credit card to the waiter. I was fed, happy, and ready to get this show on the road.

"Your card has been declined, sir", he told me.

"That's odd", I said not yet overly concerned, "there's plenty of money on there." I'm sure he'd heard this a million times from embarrassed holders of declined cards, but in this instance it was true. I had applied for the card some months earlier with the sole purpose of taking it as an emergency backup while in Japan. It had a sizable credit limit with not a penny of it yet spent. I hadn't succumbed to the near-fatal error of thinking that the credit was mine to spend, getting excited and buying stuff, just because now I could.

Credit cards frighten me. They have done ever since the 1980s, when my brother and I watched our parents lose the family home to a string of events that involved, amongst other things, naïve business choices and reckless decisions regarding credit cards: they spent money that they couldn't pay back. Credit is a modern-day evil; a necessity sometimes, but an insidious force that can cause the most heinous turmoil among families.

Look beyond the illusion of banks' smartly dressed workers, minimalist premises, and inspiring advertising campaigns, and you will see the twisted smile of a snake oil seller rubbing hands and smearing down a greasy patch of hair to one side of a sweaty brow. "Roll up, roll up little children, I have something that you will like", he might have croaked in generations before. Now he wears a shirt, tie, and burgundy brogues. He sells credit to the needy – in fact, he is prepared to increase the credit limit to those most financially vulnerable. "I'm just trying to help those who need it most", he protests.

There is no greasy patch of hair smeared to one side these days. The lawyers told him to get it cut. They said it would look better that way. People may trust him more. So I never overspend the credit on a credit card. I pay what I have spent, in full every month; and the banks hate me for it. They make no money that way, on missed payment charges and interest. And now that I can afford the increased card limit, unlike my parents before me, they don't extend me that same favour. Funny that.

Of course, Buddhist monks of old, those that have been walking the 88 temple pilgrimage since the twelfth century, did not have the luxury of a credit card. They instead opted for faith to be their go-to safety measure. Faith that life would provide guidance, security, and fortune. Maybe the snake oil sellers had never made it to the mighty wooden doorways of their temples, to tempt them with their wares. They never knew what they were missing, those Buddhists, I say. Although the pilgrimage route was old, the times are new, and credit seemed a reasonable net in which to be caught if I found myself falling.

After two more attempts and the last call for boarding, I was forced to pay my bill with cash. Credit had failed me. Now I was very concerned. Forty of a £300 cash budget (pretty much the only cash available this late in the month, with bills to pay, children to feed, and a month of no work or income ensuing) gone to placate an irate waiter twitching to call security. At the best of times, Japan is an expensive place to visit. It is costly to get to and expensive once you are there. I was now left with £260 to finance transport to and from the airport before and after the pilgrimage, food and shelter while on it, and all the things no one knows they'll need to pay for until they need to. It was now a very real possibility that I simply might not now have enough money to complete the trip.

Hope was beginning to slip away from me, and I silently cursed W. H. Murray. If you are going to publish motivational paragraphs of prose, at least make sure they work for everyone. Bastard. The roller coaster of emotions felt bipolar, the extremes exhausting. I sank into my cramped seat on board the plane and realised that I was now playing for real. I would have to walk this pilgrimage in the ways of old, mostly relying on faith to provide.

Oh heaven, help me. How on earth will this play out?

CHAPTER 4

The Darkest Night of the Soul

How to be with a now, too painful to want to face?
A biting cold.
A loss of love.
Tired legs.
—*Journal entry*

IT IS WRITTEN that, while Christ was on the cross, he called out, "My God, my God, why hast thou forsaken me?" Even Jesus felt abandoned during times of great need. St John of the Cross, a Roman Catholic mystic, elaborated on the same teaching when he wrote of the "dark night of the soul" in the sixteenth century. I was about to encounter my own dark nights here in the twenty-first.

Until now, the pilgrimage had been nothing more than an inspired decision, brimming with the thoughts, plans, and daydreams that inevitably ensue. I was excited at the prospect of embarking on a spiritual quest, an opportunity to find myself while getting lost in the process of long reflective walking. In hindsight, I suspect, part of me considered it a bit of a spiritual excursion, slightly more gruelling than an intense yoga retreat in Greece. My first night would shatter any illusions of this being a holy jolly.

The bus from the airport finally pulled into the central station of Shikoku at almost 9 p.m. The bright neon that pervades so many Japanese cities denied the night of its darkness. Noise filled space the neon couldn't infiltrate, and city smells were everywhere. I had been awake and travelling for eighteen hours, give or take the pot shots at sleep attempted on cramped plane seats, bolt upright, neck rigid, slipped discs imminent. The busy city hurt my exhausted, and now utterly congested, senses.

Japan and its culture are so unique and different from our own that it is impossible not to be bludgeoned and disoriented with their novelty. In Europe, for instance, two years of learning mandatory French at school will provide a rudimentary but useful level of understanding that can help survival in, for example, Spain, Italy, Germany, and possibly Portugal. Although each country is proud of its language, culture, and customs, the truth remains that an underpinning Europeanness is present. The countries are ultimately shades of the same colour. We share more than the things that separate us. I can hear Alessandro choking on his antipasti at my assertion that Brits and Italians are essentially the same; this fight could rage on for days, you know? He will gesticulate, a lot. I will ignore him.

Not so in Japan; its language – speaking, listening, reading, and writing – is entirely different. Japanese cuisine uses techniques and ingredients unique to its islands; their customs and culture are nearly unfathomable without decades of commitment spent unravelling them, and their religious and spiritual ideas are virtually opposites of those held in the West. Of course, in 2016 the world is now a global neighbourhood. Nothing is truly alien any longer, but Japan is as close to a unique and separate culture as it is still possible to be. On arrival, it is easy to feel suddenly lost.

While I tried to find my bearings, my Japanese legs, so to speak, I watched a couple of teenage locals busk to a small group of girls with pigtails, dressed in their short puffball skirts and knee-length socks. It's an innocent look that many Japanese girls wear, but it's an odd one.

Japan is a complicated culture filled with contradiction, juxtaposition, contrast, and surprise. In the grounds of a three-hundred-year-old Shinto temple, for instance, it is possible to find soft-drink vending machines. The beautiful veneer of Japanese food hides one of the highest rates of stomach cancer in the world. Layers of grammatical etiquette in defence of honour mask a country suffering major problems with domestic abuse and alcoholism. Aggressive Government development programmes concrete over anything that sits still for too long, at the cost of driving its natural species to the edge of extinction and beyond. The homage to nature found in so many temple gardens is a mirage – no more than a nod to what once was.

Add to all this the image of innocence represented by the "schoolgirl" look. I hate it. This look of sweetness is flaunted across sexy girl magazines and comics and hints at pornography without indulging in it. I hate it. If you are going to have a bizarre sex life, do it. Don't hint at it. Shadows create nightmares. Out in the open, we can choose to fight them, indulge them or simply ignore them. But be open. Be honest. Don't masquerade. Truth denied behind layers of deceit is a dangerous game. I hate it.

Time was pushing on, and I still needed to get from where I was at Shikoku's main station in Tokushima to the site of the pilgrimage's first and starting temple, Ryōzenji. It is traditional for pilgrims to pray at Ryōzenji for luck on their journey. It is here that they can also stock up on the plethora of spiritual accessories apparently now necessary to complete the trail: beads, bells, hats, bags, vests, maps, staff (the long stick, not the team of employees), stamp books, and stole.

I didn't know any of this before arriving. I had no idea of the depth of custom, religious etiquette, prayer, and history of the 88. I'm happy for that. Arriving in Japan with nothing more than a wish to walk its sacred walk, a general idea of manners necessary to survive there, and a rucksack filled with my stuff, I was ready to learn on the move.

Looking for the next connecting bus, I turned to a call from a cab that pulled up alongside me to ask if I needed a ride. Still smarting from my severely depleted budget during the credit card fiasco, I had to decline politely and ask the cab driver if he knew where to stand for the next bus.

"Where are you going?" asked the cabby.

"Ryōzenji Temple. I'm going to walk the *hachi jū hachi. Watashi wa Henro desu.*" I told him I was a pilgrim – a *Henro* – and I was here to walk the 88.

"You get bus around the *Henro Michi?*" (Locals often refer to the 88 as the pilgrims' road, the *Henro Michi*.)

"Iie, aruite." I told him that, no, I would walk the 1,400 kilometres.

He ordered me into his cab, drove me the forty minutes to Ryōzenji, bowed before he left, and didn't charge me a penny. I wondered if W. H. Murray's book had reached these far-off islands. Maybe Providence was waving her hand after all.

At this late hour I found the temple and all its administrative buildings closed until morning, despite hoping that God would cut me some slack and the temple would stay open, just for me; I was a foreigner in a foreign land after all. This was the first of many delusions. Apparently, even gods have to sleep, and I would have to wait until morning to begin the 88.

Japanese Buddhism teaches much about delusion being one cause of unhappiness. I had supposed that I might receive some special treatment – divinely inspired perhaps. Here I was, entirely deluded and quite unhappy about it. Buddha was right. Uncanny. My first night in Japan, my first night on the sacred 88 temple pilgrimage, wasn't quite going to plan. After eighteen hours in transit and now more than three thousand miles from home, I was shattered. My mind ached, I was famished, the temple gates were closed, and I didn't have the budget for a meal and a night's lodging. This would be my first night living on the streets. At first, it seems manageable, six or so hours to survive until the morning and the warmth of a new day, but the first of two problems arises. Boredom.

At home, from around 8 or 9 p.m. until bedtime, the evening is filled with making dinner, watching TV, reading, having a bath, working on a project, doing homework, listening to music, until, feeling the day draw to a close, heavy eyelids encourage us to bed. Sitting on the stone steps at the locked gates of Ryōzenji, all I had was a backpack of minimal supplies (as advised by one of the four paragraphs that my Rough Guide dedicated to the journey). Of entertainment value were a small notebook and pen and a video camera. I had chosen to bring both as means of documenting the trip in some way.

When there is nothing to do, time drags with mind-bending

tardiness; it bends further, it seems, to appear even slower when one desperately wants it to speed up and pass. Addiction to activity in our modern lives makes it very hard to be alone doing nothing. I spent summers in the 1970s playing for endless hours with simple things: a cardboard box, mud and sand, a broken bike. Nowadays we have "evolved" into an era where every gadget, activity, or pastime has been created so that we don't have to suffer the trauma of long periods alone traversing dark nights of the soul. When alone with nothing to do, the untethered mind is free to reel. And I think that frightens many of us.

Exposure to this chattering mind is one of the supposed benefits of pilgrimage. With little else to distract, it is possible finally to fully witness the plethora of mental noise that tumbles and streams through our minds. Ideas, memories, doubts, fantasies, plans, goals, desires, regrets, fears, resentments – thoughts seemingly spring from nowhere to pull at our attention. On pilgrimage we have the time, the space, and the opportunity to address the voices, many of which seem unsolicited, and we can begin to ask: Who is doing the thinking? Who am I? Am I more than this, less than this? Each thought contains the potential for the next, like the threads of a spider's web. Each idea links to, and provides support for, the subsequent silky attachment. Thought after thought, thread after thread, create a new structure, a web, a new belief, a mind stuffed with more ideas. Endless mental chatter feels relentless, untidy, and uncomfortable. It is exhausting. Often I find myself shifting from one foot to another to escape the multitude of mental intrusions that I seem unable to outrun or solve. They are, however, inescapable.

On this first night alone, the internal noise seemed magnified. In fact, it was just the movement of thinking, from background to foreground, forced by the silence of inactivity.

The second of the night's challenges was cold. During February at night in rural Japan, it is incredibly cold. Ordinarily, as the sun starts to set, heating is switched on, and we never truly suffer the natural temperature change of the day, even for a moment. Why would we? It is the twenty-first century, after all. Why bother feeling the bone aching cold of a winter's night when we have evolved our lives so successfully away from such discomforts? We are working toward the peak of Maslow's triangular psychological hierarchy of needs: upward growth from physiological needs at its base through safety, love, and esteem to self-actualization, finally, at its peak. Why go backwards, we are evolving beings after all? I would urge everyone to experience living a full day without the comforts of modernity. Not as a protest against modernity – I love home comforts – but as a means of appreciating the natural rhythms of the day. We all know the sun warms the earth; every child learns this in the earliest grades of school. But to feel it is a different thing. It is as contrasting as visiting a lion in a zoo and then watching the same beast on the plains of Botswana. Both are life, but one shines brighter than the other.

Walking the 88, as monks of the past did, you are forced to live the rhythms of the day. It is not an exaggeration to say that your survival could depend on them. In the early afternoon, the falling sun is gradual; it is easy to ignore. But when the last of the light disappears behind a distant horizon, the drop in temperature is sudden. The dramatic change always evokes a response, a zipping up of a jacket or the automatic stuffing of hands in pockets. However, the night has several levels of cold. Midnight to around 2.00 would prove to be my mental nemesis.

It was on my first night that I would be duly acquainted with this "dead of night". With little else to do, my mind had nothing on which to fixate other than the cold and dark working their way deep into my bones and thoughts. By now I was wearing every piece of clothing from my backpack to ward off the penetrating freeze, my resistance to the discomfort only seeming to intensify it. Out in the sticks, silence couples late dark hours. Sometimes it is terrifying. Nothing moves, sings, or is animate at this time, and it feels the way I imagine oblivion to be. Even the long hours that birds keep do not extend into the dead of night. They *cheep-cheep* until late and will sing again at dawn, but even they hide from these hours of the void. They refused to keep me company in this morbid dark.

I don't like the dark. I haven't since trying to emulate my older brother's love for horror shows and films back in the days of *Hammer House of Horrors*, *Tales of the Unexpected*, *The Omen*, and *Carrie*. I hated anything even remotely scary but, like many younger siblings, idolised my brother, older by four years. And I was prepared to scar my young mind to meet his approval.

It is easy to understand how stories of ghosts and strange things are born and intensified in the hours of dark. It feels like death, and I would have to face this spectre many times while on pilgrimage, this one just an introduction. I wandered off in search of somewhere suitable to rest and get warm.

Rice is a staple of the Japanese diet. There are vending machines in many towns used to clean and shell unprocessed grain that locals buy in bulk. Metal shacks with sliding doors shelter customers and their rice from the weather as they pour their rice through the machines. They are open twenty-four hours a day, 365 days of the year. It was in one of these that I tried to find sleep and warmth. Cold and exhaustion had almost paralysed me by the time I found this refuge. I fell asleep on a hard wooden bench used for holding bulk bags of rice, used my backpack as a pillow (somewhat depleted now that I was wearing almost its entire contents), and collapsed into sleep. Pain in my back woke me forty minutes later. Although not crippling, it was severe enough that I couldn't take any more. I needed to stretch and find somewhere else to spend the rest of the night. Just the tiniest amount of this long night had passed.

Wandering back to Ryōzenji, I hoped that I'd previously somehow missed a perfect place to rest – an open room, an unlocked door, or perhaps a sheltered alcove. I hadn't. God was not budging tonight. Ryōzenji would not be my refuge. With nowhere better to rest, cold and pain in my back (and backside), I decided that I might as well get on and start walking the damn pilgrimage there and then. At least walking would keep me warm. To hell with the commencement ceremony, rituals, and pilgrim paraphernalia. I couldn't afford it anyhow.

So my pilgrimage had formally begun, though not as expected; honestly, I wasn't sure what I expected. I was forced to do the only thing I knew how: take the first steps of the first mile of a very long journey, one foot in front of the other.

CHAPTER 5

Meeting Thy Maker

One step.
—*Journal entry*

TEMPLES 1 THROUGH 10 are situated relatively close to one another at the beginning of the 88, just a mile or two separating successive shrines. As dawn finally broke the night, the miles of walking piled up as I weaved my way along this network of Buddhist sites. The gentle curves of temple roofs with their dark woods, faded greens, and elaborate golds became clearer as daylight pierced the predawn grey. I watched early worshippers come and go, performing morning rituals in front of altars before heading off to work. Sunlight bounced off golden Buddhas looking on from within temple gardens.

I knew nothing of formal Buddhist custom at this point, aside from the translation of it that pervades Western perspective. Everything witnessed at these early stages was a brand-new lesson. I was a total beginner with a blank canvas of ignorance.

In his book *Zen Mind, Beginner's Mind*, Japanese author and *Zen* Buddhist monk Shunryū Suzuki teaches the importance of bringing a beginner's mind to our lives. "In the beginner's mind, there are many possibilities, in the expert's mind there are few", he teaches. Guarding against the restrictions of an expert's mind was hardly a problem I needed to fear. You can accuse me of many things, but being an expert is not one of them.

As I trekked onwards towards Fujiidera, Temple 11, the temples

I had already visited faded into the distance behind. Until now my fatigue had been diverted by their myriad distractions, each temple unique, fascinating, and celebrating a particular deity, ideal, or aspect of Buddhism. But now, wide open spaces, farmland, and rice fields offered none for the next twelve miles or so, and I soon began to feel incredibly tired. I had been walking for just a single morning, covering less than one percent of the total distance, and already I was utterly shattered, physically and mentally. These, however, were just a couple of the obstacles I would be facing.

Part of the purpose of the trip was to put a sock in the mouths of people who complain that time and money, or rather the lack of them, will limit life's potential. Fear wouldn't allow me to buy into these complaints. What a grim reality this would turn out to be if it were true. In that case, optimism, courage, hope, and the joy of shooting for the stars would be crushed.

Is the rat race the highest goal life can muster for us? Really? I needed to prove that this wasn't so, as much for my benefit as theirs, and the 88 would be my testing ground. Like all experiments, this one had to begin with a hypothesis to either prove or disprove through observation and analysis. The ultimate conclusion would confirm yea or nay, heaven or hell:

- Heaven if yes, time and money were poor human choices, but not universally binding certainties; heaven if, in fact, we are totally free, indeed encouraged, to live the life of our dreams. Whoopee! What a comforting discovery this would be.
- Hell, however, if time and money scarcity were all that the gods had planned for us; hell if they enjoyed looking down from their ambrosial thrones at our struggles with abundance, pain, frustration, hope, fear, and dull, tedious lives. Hell, if they enjoyed playing us like pawns in a heavenly version of the Hunger Games.

The guidebooks suggest four to six weeks to walk the 88; some even suggest splitting it into two separate trips. Other advisers instruct that a budget ten times the amount I had in my pocket is needed to complete the journey safely. My empirical reasoning was simple: If I could achieve my dream (walking the 88) despite having insufficient money (£260) or time (return plane ticket to London in thirty days), then I could demonstrate that these limitations need not bind us. I would show that life was bigger than the mental limits we impose on ourselves and that the heavens are actually on our side, willing us on to the lives of our dreams. If only we knew it was allowed.

Although clearly this was not a laboratory test – I wasn't even wearing a white coat – I planned to document my findings and experiences both on a video camera and in a journal. Right now, though, hellish conclusions were looking more likely than heavenly. I had calculated that I would need to walk the equivalent of a marathon and a half, every day, for the next thirty days to finish on time. I had walked just twelve miles so far and was already in pieces. I'd already had enough and, effectively, only reached the end of the drive!

And then it got worse.

It wasn't until after this that I learned that the walk between Temples 11 and 12 (Fujiidera to Shōsanji) is considered one of the most challenging stretches of the entire pilgrimage. A heads-up would have been most welcome. The pilgrim is eased in, or teased, early on with flat lands, encouraging a false sense of security to prevail. The path then shoots skyward up mountain trails at gradients that thump the heart, drain the legs, and cloud the spirit. Six hours of brutal terrain and the fear of being caught on the mountainside at day's end, as light begins to fade, add strain to the shattering effort it takes to manage even one foot ahead of the other.

Reality had replaced daydreaming by now, and I was left wondering if my task was achievable. Suddenly, it all seemed too much. I felt entirely overwhelmed and started to oscillate between fear and anger. The trails were getting ever steeper, and my resistance made it worse. In the clutches of anger bouts, it was easy to imagine Buddhist deities laughing at me. Descending negativity was squeezing my clarity of mind and positivity.

Life has a peculiar logic, it seems. Finally, I reached the crest of the climb. I had arrived at the base of a beautiful ancient cedar tree, its canopy shading the statue of a pilgrim and a bench on which at first I sat and then slumped into a deep sleep. I woke up lying on my back and looking up into the face of a pilgrim statue that held rosary beads in one hand and a staff in another. The soft faded browns and greens of the copper sculpture blended with the natural colours of the cedar tree canopy. The statue was of Kōbō Daishi, the eighth Patriarch of the Shingon sect of Buddhism and founder of the 88 temple pilgrimage. Often referred to as Kūkai (774–835) by locals who hold him close to their hearts, Kōbō Daishi was actively spreading Buddhism throughout Japan and is a key religious figure from its history. The Japanese say that Kūkai is always with his pilgrims while on the 88, protecting them. In Japanese they call it *Dōgyō-ninin*, "same practice, two people" being the exact translation. The benevolent monk is always present for support and comfort.

Who knows if this is true or not, but I felt at ease here, at his feet amidst the creaking of old trees and the gentle sounds of nature. The temperature was cold except for the warmth of sun slithers that found my face through the branches. The nap that I'd enjoyed, this beautiful place and maybe also Kōbō Daishi had revived me. I was calm now, profoundly peaceful, and refreshed. It was time to press on again. I had a pilgrimage to walk.

As brutal and challenging as these mountainous trails had been, they had provided the first vital lesson of the 88: When overwhelmed with a task seemingly too large to handle, concentrate on just the next step. Earlier, I was too busy complaining about the magnitude of the steep climbs and fearing what was to come to realise this first lesson. But now my head was clear, and it was obvious: Put your head down and focus on the one step that you are walking, right here, right now at this moment. It's all you can ever really do, when you consider it. I named this process one-stepping, and I started to apply it to everything and anything challenging. I wondered if maybe Kūkai had a hand in helping me understand.

CHAPTER 6

Mr Beginnings

Trust means to let go.
—*Journal entry*

BUDDHISTS TEACH THAT life is a continuous cycle of life and death. Each moment draws to a close only to be replaced by the birth of another. Beginnings eventually end to free the path for further beginnings.

By now I had been walking several days since beginning at Ryōzenji Temple miles before. But my pilgrimage would start anew after I met Mr Beginnings. His name was Hajime-san. *Hajime*, in Japanese, means to begin; *San*, the equivalent honorific to Mr or Mrs. His name translates as Mr Beginnings! I had reached Jōrakuji, Temple 14, and the pain from my walking boots was unbearable; this did not bode well for the seventy-four temples left to visit. My brand-new highly recommended Karrimors lay scattered as I relieved my feet of their tyranny.

"Too heavy", he barked, picking up one of my discarded boots and waving it in my face. "Why you here?"

It is sometimes difficult to decipher the intention behind the front of a Japanese. Generations of social hierarchy and politeness, overpopulated land space, the need to protect privacy, and a culture that abhors embarrassment or disgrace have all led to people who give little away through facial expression; the ultimate poker face.

"Um, I'm here to walk the *hachi jū hachi*." With my limited

Japanese I tried the best I could to explain my intentions to this fierce interrogating stranger.

"You know Hannya Shingyō?" Hajime-san snapped.

"No." I didn't. I didn't even know what he'd just said. He spotted my confusion.

"Hannya Shingyō, Hannya Shingyō?" he barked. He looked like he might bite too. I shook my head in shame – although I wasn't sure what I was supposed to feel shame about.

"Come", he ordered for me to follow. Seemingly, I couldn't refuse.

I followed him to the main hall of the temple, skulking behind like a naughty schoolboy. Just before the main altar he stopped, reached into his backpack, pulled out a *kyōhon* – a book of sutras – and thrust it into my hand.

"This is the Hannya Shingyō. Hannya Shingyō is why you do the *hachi* jū *hachi*. You read *nihongo*, Japanese?"

"Yes, a little." Hajime san's angry face broke briefly into a toothless smile. I bathed momentarily in his silent congratulations, relieved that I had said something that didn't anger him further. The Japanese love it if you show you understand and can speak a little of their language or try to. They also enjoy a foreigner's resignation to their truth that Japan is the best country on the planet. Ever. Much better than ours.

"Good." With prayer beads held between clasped hands, Hajime-san proceeded to chant. I watched him and listened, starry-eyed in admiration, until he stopped suddenly. "Begin", he ordered.

Oh god! He wanted me to follow along. I could read the *hiragana* - one of the two Japanese phonetic alphabets (the other being *Katakana* for foreign and imported words) - but not at the speed he was chanting. I began to sweat. He continued, with an air of furious expectancy and without looking at me. No more silent congratulations for me.

Hannya Shingyō is the Japanese name for the heart sutra. It is the said to be the most important, popular and best known of all Buddhist works and makes up part of the liturgy performed at temple altars. Kōbō Daishi is believed to have taught that the sutra's frequent recitation would lead worshippers to enlightenment. I stumbled along with Hajime-san, panicking at his harsh gestures that coincided with my mistakes. After three recitals, it was over. The new look he gave was not of approval. It suggested that he thought perhaps he had chosen to mentor an idiot – one who probably couldn't be helped, in this life or the next!

"*Ikimashō* – let's go." Off to the next temple we went. My apprenticeship with Hajime-san, it seemed, had begun. Whether I wanted it or not.

The days that followed would teach me the true meaning and purpose of walking the *hachi jū hachi* as well as life lesson number three. After making a committed decision to chase dreams and breaking down the immensity of the task into baby steps, one at a time, there often comes a point when you simply don't have the knowledge to overcome the next obstacle. It happens to the very best of us. As I followed on after my new leader, the saying "When the student is ready, the teacher will appear" sprang to mind. I started to wonder if maybe my meeting with Hajime-san had a little of the providential flavour that W. H. Murray had spoken of in his prose. Had Hajime-san been sent to teach me the proper foundations of the 88? Coincidence or divine intervention?

The whole of the first day that Hajime came into my life was spent perfecting the Hannya Shingyō at each of the temples we visited. The training was the same; he would chant, and I was expected to follow correctly. Slowly but surely, under such intense scrutiny, I started to get it. Occasional grunts of approval encouraged me. Regular scorn discouraged error. It never occurred to me that I was following a total stranger; never even popped into my head. It was as if this was just the way it was meant to be. This man would plant seeds in my mind that are still blossoming today.

In the middle of the day, we stopped at a supermarket to pick up some lunch. Hajime unloaded his backpack and left it outside in the car park. I kept mine on my back. "What are you doing?" he said, pointing at my backpack.

"Someone might take it," I answered.

"Mattō-san, leave it here."

It was an innocuous order that didn't register until much later. I did as Hajime said because it felt as though he was in charge. It was only much further into the pilgrimage I realised another essential lesson: trust. To trust means to let go. I noted this flash of insight into my notebook: to be able to let go of fear and the need to control. Paradoxically, letting go is the very thing that seems to ensure security. The everyday act of leaving my backpack in the car park while we shopped for lunch would play havoc with my mind, but it also began to shake the belief system on which this chaos fed. *Let go* was the lesson. *Trust* was the command.

My thoughts trailed back through the years. My daughter, India, aged three and in nursery school, had a biting problem. If other children gave her a problem, she bit them. It was the last meeting with the senior nursery staff that left me in despair. India had used up all her chances. She would have to stop, or she would no longer be welcome at 'Busy bees-where youngsters learn to grow'. Expelled at three! Not the start to life I had planned for her. Since the last two warnings, I had tried everything to get her to stop. Nothing seemed to work. There was nothing further I could do as a parent, and she would have to take her licks, as in boxing, the way I did as a youngster, years before her. It was hard to resign myself to such an outlook, but the moment I accepted this possible fate and relaxed into the difficulties it might present, she stopped her biting stage, literally overnight. Life works like this, it seems. My daughter stopped biting, and my backpack was safe; trust and acceptance are powerful tools.

Through a combination of broken English and elementary Japanese, I came to learn a little about Hajime's life. He had lost his entire family in a car accident some time before and had been walking the *hachi jū hachi* ever since. When finished, he would start all over. I wondered if the circle would ever end for him. Did his grief grow easier with each circumambulation of the Island of Shikoku?

People walk the 88 for a multitude of reasons. I met many along the way, each with different goals. A student on extended holiday wanted to do something spiritual and notable for his CV. A lady in her twenties was praying for the full recovery of a sister with ovarian cancer. A "salaryman" (the name the Japanese use for office nine-to-fivers) in his fifties was looking to find life meaning beyond the confines of Japanese corporate dictates.

The sun started to set, and our day of walking and praying was coming to a close. I wondered where we would stay for the night. "On the streets, as a proper *Henro*," he would say, sleeping where sleep found us, as pilgrims and spiritual seekers; two homeless men by any other name.

We found the nearest bus shelter, made of chunky pinewood, two benches, and a corrugated roof. I watched him unpack some of all the life belongings he carried with him on his never-ending pilgrimage: mini gas canister, two small tin bowls, cups, and unfathomable packets of dried food provisions. He was going to cook us dinner, by candlelight, in a bus shelter. With an old-fashioned battery powered radio playing softly in the corner, we dined. The light of the candle flickered warm shadows against the walls, and billions of stars spotted the vast canvas of sky outside.

My eyes grew heavy and ached to close, in that lovely drifting way. I felt strangely at home with this man of the road who was teaching me the ways of the 88. Even so, I silently prayed that he wouldn't kill me in my sleep. The doubts of a neurotic Westerner were not quite walked out of me yet.

My painfully rigid back awoke me. Hard wooden benches had a habit of doing that, it seemed. Hajime was still asleep, and I was still alive. Thank God. I stepped outside to stretch. A new day on the 88. I needed to press on with the miles today. I was falling behind my daily quota and wouldn't reach my final goal at this rate. I wondered when Hajime would wake. He did eventually, and I tried to explain my walking goals with subtlety, in a language of which I had only a rudimentary grasp. "One step, Mattō-san" was his only answer.

On this day Hajime gave me a set of Buddhist prayer beads and added them to our rituals of chanting and bowing at each temple. I was to twist them gently with my middle fingers into a folded figure of eight, a symbol of eternity and the never-ending cycle of life, the samsaric existence from which we were praying to be freed. I held them while reciting the prayer. After we finished, he taught me to wear them around my wrist until using them again at our next destination.

"Hungry, Mattō-san?" Hajime asked me late in the afternoon. I was. Famished. We were walking through the city of Tokushima after temporarily leaving mountainous countryside behind. The 88 offers a constant contrast between town and country, up and down, steep and flat, challenging and straightforward, all perfectly expressed within the yin-yang symbol of Far Eastern traditional medicine, philosophy, and some religions.

This interesting symbol is often slightly misunderstood in the West. Two equal-sized teardrops, reminiscent of the famous paisley pattern, equally divide a circle. One is black; the other is white. In the black teardrop is a dot of white; in the white, a dot of black. The dots are important; don't underestimate their significance. They represent the lesson that darkness contains the birth of light, as light provides the delivery of dark, a never-ending cycle of change and transformation.

Many believe that the black symbol represents male qualities and the white, female ones. This understanding is partially right. Advanced readings of the symbol teach that the symbols represent relativity. Black (yang) can only be black in the presence of white (yin); up (yang), can only be up in the presence of down (yin). This level of comprehension teaches us about interdependence and coexistence: something only exists along with something else. We need others to be who we are.

We headed into a side street, through a sliding door, and into a noodle bar. The man behind the counter seemed delighted to see Hajime, a regular at his restaurant on long and homeless days. The food was served for us both, without being ordered, cheap but delicious and fulfilling; a bowl of ramen noodles and miso soup, Japanese staple fare. I was struggling to coordinate the prayer beads around my wrist and the eating of my meal. Each time I dipped the wooden ladle into the bowl, the ends of the beads threatened to follow it into the soup. I took them off to put around my neck until I felt a sharp and sudden hand on my arm: "No, Mattō-san!" barked Hajime. I froze on the spot. "Never, *ever* put prayer beads around your neck!" he admonished.

I was both embarrassed and a little shaken at his sudden and severe tone. I hadn't meant to upset my mentor. "I'm so sorry, Hajime-san," I apologised, not knowing the significance of my blunder.

"It's OK, Mattō-san, you did not know." He went on to explain that in wars gone by, captors identified Buddhist monks by the prayer beads on their wrists.

In war, it is a common tactic for captors to deny people their religion, to steal their faith, solace, and last vestiges of hope. History is littered with examples of invasions and subsequent religious conversions, at best, or death and spiritual quelling, at worst. Japanese Buddhists had suffered the same fate in past times: captured and led away, those to be beheaded were identified by the beads that had been removed from their wrists and hung around their necks. Ever since, it has been considered bad luck for anyone to do the same with their prayer beads. I was learning, minute by minute on the streets, from within the depths of Japan. My guide could be no better.

After dinner, it was time to be schooled in another consideration for the pilgrim: bathing. We arrived downtown outside a building that you would stay away from if you were not with someone "in the know": old, tattered, and threatening (the building, not Hajime, although now that I think about it …). I followed Hajime inside. The lighting was grim and depressing, and darkened corners showed where broken bulbs had been left unchanged. Undefinable and unpleasant smells permeated everywhere. He had brought me to a public *onsen*.

Onsen is the Japanese word for hot baths. Entailing ritual and rule, it is a delicious and delightful tradition of Japan, much the way it is in Scandinavia. You ignore them at your peril. A precise rinsing sequence follows an equally meticulous washing routine. Then, and only then, are you permitted to enter the large hot baths that help melt life's tensions. Japan is a country and culture of ritual, detail, etiquette, and manners. To ignore their rituals flagrantly is the highest level of discourtesy and is a sure-fire way to make your experience in Japan a difficult one. Bathing and its associated rules are some of the most important rituals to get right.

But this was no ordinary *onsen*. This one seemed to be just for the poor and homeless. I don't know if this was by design or by default, but I was relieved that I was with a Japanese on my first run here.

Old men filled the changing rooms. They might not have been old, but extended life on the streets made them seem so. None looked up as we entered, save for a couple, all others keeping themselves to themselves and inside their worlds and barricades. Privacy: another aspect of this land that foreigners must honour. Those who stole a glance glared accusingly at me, a *gaijin* (foreigner), until Hajime barked something at them, and they returned to their business. It seemed now that Hajime had cleared the way, and I could get on and enjoy those marvellous hot baths.

After a long day walking the roads, the hot and nourishing baths were like heaven on earth. I'd never appreciated such a simple a pleasure so much. As tensions relaxed, I even became momentary entertainment for some of these homeless men sharing the *onsen* that evening. They pointed at my muscles and my penis and chuckled at the differences between them and me, a foreigner. I wasn't sure if they were impressed or not. It was funny all the same. The atmosphere was easing as the water warmed muscles. They started to forget that there was a stranger in their midst.

I was experiencing just a sliver of time as a homeless person, as Hajime's apprentice on the 88, but for many of these men, it was their permanent residence: life on the streets forced by circumstances gone awry. I read somewhere that we are all just one thread from being homeless; emotional, financial, or family tragedy is enough to send many to a life of destitution. This brief time on the streets was enough to help me appreciate how lucky my life is and to consider more deeply those whose lives are not so.

I have been fortunate enough to experience the juxtaposition of rich and poor at other times in my life too. As a professional tennis coach in my twenties, I taught in an exclusive London-based private members' club in the morning and drove to teach underprivileged school children attending poorly funded schools in the afternoon. My mornings were very often spent teaching celebrity and royalty, and my afternoons teaching day-to-day-children. Perfect and poor behaviour existed in both camps; they were children after all. What I learnt most was this: those who had little sneered at those who had much. Those who had much were afraid of the coarseness of those who had little. The funny thing was, neither side had any direct experience of the other. I did, thankfully, and I realised that both sides were practically identical in their needs, desires, fears, and passions. The money they had in their lives was just a number.

Re-energised by the *onsen*, Hajime and I headed back into the burgeoning night. It was time to rest, and he knew of a *tsūyadō* one hour's walk further on. Along the 88 it is possible to find *tsūyadō*s if you know where to look. A *tsūyadō* is a small hut or building for pilgrims to rest temporarily and shelter. Local communities contribute money and skills to build them so that the arduous journey of pilgrims is slightly easier to bear. This offering, as a way of thanks for a pilgrim's effort, is called *takahatsu*. Temporary shelter, a *tsūyadō*, is one example; gifts and food are others. *Tsūyadō* is a most welcomed offering, particularly at the end of a long, wet day.

The Japanese value highly both the 88 temple pilgrimage and its pilgrims. The generous offering of a *tsūyadō* is an important indicator of how much. The hardship endured by pilgrims is not solely for the betterment of their life by lessons learnt along the way. Pilgrims face difficulties for the betterment of everybody's life through the sharing of lessons learnt along the way. It is a beautiful idea that makes Buddhism such an appealing concept: the idea of paying forward knowledge, merit, and positive attributes attained. It is summed up in a Buddhist prayer preceding formal meditation:

> *May all beings have happiness and create the causes and*
> *conditions of happiness,*
> *May they be free from suffering and free from creating the*
> *causes of suffering,*
> *May they achieve that noble happiness that can never be*
> *tainted by suffering,*
> *And may they achieve universal impartial compassion*
> *beyond worldly bias towards friends or enemies.*

Giving is an interesting subject that throws up controversial issues. Giving can be lazy, little more than a financial assuager of guilt, a few coins tossed onto the offering plate at the end of a church service. Be honest, if you weren't under watchful eyes, would you bother? But effort spent for the benefit of another is an altogether different thing: the marathon runner pounding the streets in a chicken costume to raise money for leukaemia research; the volunteers who sit with senior citizens, no longer with a family, three afternoons a week, despite hearing the same old stories over and over; the sacrifice of a precious Saturday afternoon to help a mate move flats; and, of course, the building and offering of shelter. "Actions speak louder than pounds" is my new version of an old classic. Of course, real givers often stay amidst the shadows. I never met most who offered me shelter while on the 88. To those, I'd like to thank you. *Dōmo arigatō gozaimasu*, just in case you are reading this in Japan.

It was the rain that woke me the next morning, hammering on the tin roof of the shack. The day was monotone, grey and uninspiring; heavy cloud cover dulled the sound outside, falling rain splashed in already deep puddles. Hajime did not like the wet. He would tolerate and walk in any weather except rain. He said that it was bad, and it made you ill if you got damp. Being wet and damp was a street dweller's worst nightmare, worse than the cold.

I remember being told the same thing at a church-run Christmas hostel for the homeless back in the UK. After serving dinner, local volunteers would chat with the guests and get to know them. Some longed for the company, others wanted you to "leave them the fuck alone", but all had stories of lives before their homelessness. The line between secure and destitute is a very fine and frail one, another thing that Buddha apparently taught; small choices or circumstance are often the divider.

So while it was raining, we would remain under cover. As the rains continued to tap on the metal sheet throughout the morning, I lay on my tatami drifting in and out of sleep, hypnotised by its steady rhythm. It was a slothful but very lovely morning except for a nagging thought that I really should be making tracks. I was losing time I didn't have.

Hajime was across the room working on something. He was deep in concentration, his glasses worn low on his nose, alternating looks both through the lenses and then over the top, squinting. I didn't want to disturb him, but I really wanted to know what he was doing, so I bum-shuffled to sit next to him and watch.

On a piece of card no bigger than A5, in a mixture of both Sanskrit and Japanese, he was writing out the Hannya Shingyō from memory. I have never seen such detailed craftsmanship. It was beautiful, and it left me speechless.

The practice of copying sutra is called *shakyō* in Japan. It is a Buddhist practice that combines the art of Japanese calligraphy (*shōdō*) and Buddhist prayer. Writing the prayer, as does its recital, is taught as a route to an enlightened state. *Shakyō* is said to harmonise both mind and body, and the teachings are absorbed with little resistance while in this state. Irrespective of its religious or spiritual benefits, it is an art that is skilful, beautiful, and transfixing, both for observer and artist.

I was happy. Relaxed and happy. Except for the nagging thought that with every moment that passed, I was losing ground on a pilgrimage that needed to be completed to prove my hypothesis that we are unlimited. That was the long and the short of it. With a time limit in place, I had no time to lose. I wasn't even confident I could complete the walk even within the perfect walking schedule I had planned in my mind.

Hajime recognised my uneasiness. "One step, Mattō-san," was all he said, and he went back to his calligraphy. I had considered the lesson of "one step" for several days: the teaching of mindful living in the present moment. Neither stuck in the past nor desirous of the future, but resting acceptingly in the only time and moment we have: now.

Lessons can be ironic. We often acknowledge their value, theoretically, but for whatever reason sometimes we are neither ready nor able as yet to apply them to our lives. Years of living a competitive, goal-driven youth had permeated my being, even though I ached to be transformed by this pilgrimage. I continued to watch Hajime. Immersed in what he was doing, he looked unshakably peaceful. He had nowhere to get to, after all. I envied that. I did need to get somewhere though, and this was the truth of my present reality. Desirous or not, I had a trip to complete.

After a few hours, I had decided I would have to press on into the rain, with or without Hajime-san. He was my mentor, but we were at different stages in our lives, and no matter how unevolved I suspected I was being, I had to finish this bloody pilgrimage on time and budget. How would I tell my spiritual guide that I was going? It would clearly demonstrate that his protégé had not absorbed his "one step" advice.

Hajime-san interrupted my thoughts. "Mattō-san, you must go. It's OK. You must go. I have a present for you." He handed me the small piece of a card he had been preparing for me all morning. He had known this moment was coming. "You must remember the real heart of the *hachi jū hachi*, Mattō-san – the Hannya Shingyō." With that, he bowed deeply, opened the sliding doors to the road, and sent me on my way.

The sky was still grey as I left my mentor of the 88, and I cried. I walked and cried until the sun finally peeked from behind clouds many miles later.

CHAPTER 7

The Miracle of Mindfulness

"I am not this",
Mooed the laughing cow amongst the sheep,
"Unless, of course, I want to be."
—*Journal entry*

MINDFULNESS HAS BECOME a bit of a buzzword on the high street. Everywhere I go, I see it. On a coffee shop noticeboard is a flyer for a "course in mindfulness"; the local fitness centre holds regular "mindfulness sessions". My Facebook feed spits out daily memes with mindfulness quoted somewhere in them, and if I want to, I could buy enough mindfulness colouring books to last me a lifetime – longer if I coloured within the lines. It's the latest feel-good fad. It worries me that, like all fads, its deep and essential importance will be overlooked by the masses moving on to the next great thing. I hope this doesn't happen. Allow me to go out on a limb and say this: wide-scale mindfulness practice could facilitate the beginnings of world peace. I realise it is an ambitious statement, but Lord knows, we need to try something.

I was first introduced to the concept of mindfulness when I was seventeen and running full tilt at a career in professional tennis. It was a path I was so committed to pursuing that the school's careers officer cancelled our mandatory sixth form appointment. The officer wished me luck and made me promise to send a signed photo if I made it big, his only request for not dragging me through a portfolio of possible careers that I would have hated. I never sent him the photo, because I never made it big. When beset with a tennis player's worst nightmare – a fragile mind – it's nigh on impossible to break into the world's top hundred tennis rankings. A weak mental game is as bad news to an aspiring tennis pro as a glass jaw is to a boxer; all other positive attributes are overshadowed by this weakest link.

My parents signed me up for sessions with a sports psychologist. Twice a week dad would traipse with me to Southfields to sit in her therapy room, which I remember being dazzling. Too bright. She even had a brown leather sofa for me to lie on while she talked me through her therapies. It didn't work. I was never calmed by the sports psychologist, as her saccharine voice talked me down an imaginary escalator of relaxation to my "happy place". Positive affirmations in front of a mirror never stuck, and my upbringing was hardly troublesome (how many parents would fork out £120 an hour for uncertain therapies?). I continued to lose tennis matches, bottling the big points and losing my temper on others.

If nothing else, though, it did spark a fascination with the workings of the mind. My journey of self-study had started, and my reading began with a book called *The Inner Game of Tennis* by Timothy Gallwey. It was a book that made me feel understood. This guy was talking about things that had happened to me, and it normalised them. Maybe I wasn't crazy after all. At some stage, I started to see that the mind games in sport are just a reflection of the same ones played out in life. I learnt that I could apply the lessons of a tennis court in other areas, too.

I'm not religious, but I am a believer, in something as yet undefined, and so it wasn't long before the New Age genre, and personal growth departments of bookshops grabbed my attention. Departments may be overstating it. In reality, they are often the smallest and dingiest spaces in the shop, far enough away from mainstream customers buying more credible titles so they are not scared off by the weirdos indulging their guilty pleasures. There is a lot of good work contained in the books of these genres, but there is an awful lot of utter drivel too. I know, I've waded through enough of them to get to the gems. The trouble is that the information is almost impossible to authenticate. When challenged, New Age teachers often offer clichéd defences such as "If it doesn't work for you, you are not ready/you haven't tried enough/it is not your path". Could it be that they are just writing nonsense? They do their genre more harm than good with such prosaic responses.

Usually, right next door to the cubbyholes that contain New Age titles are the religious ones. Even smaller than the growing New Age genre, nevertheless it is slightly more credible standing in front of the Bible than *The 7 Laws of feeling super-duper*. At the very least, religion has been proselytising long enough to have worked on its message, even if much of it is misguided. Whether you like what religions preach or not, they have stuck to their guns. It was in the religious section that I found *The Tibetan Book of Living and Dying* by Sogyal Rinpoche. It is a book about the teachings of Tibetan Buddhism. Sogyal Rinpoche is one of the leading lights of Tibetan Buddhism, and only the Dalai Lama is ranked higher. I read the book from cover to cover. Some of it I understood, some was beyond me; some of it bored me, some was eye opening. One particular section inspired me, the part about mindfulness meditation. Just as Gallwey had spoken directly to me through *The Inner Game of Tennis*, Sogyal Rinpoche was now personally inviting me to engage in something that could change my life forever.

Mindfulness is an incredible skill that sits at the heart of Buddhism. Walking the 88 helps cultivate it to profound levels, and it's not as esoteric as you might think. Most of us criticise and doubt what we misunderstand. It's a human trait. But the belief that mindfulness practice is some outdated Far Eastern, Voodoo mind control was debunked long ago. It is a skill as relevant for today's Western living as it was for Eastern households of yesteryear.

I hesitate to use the term *Western life*; it's a phrase that feels as if it should have died with the last vestiges of communism. No longer is the world split so decisively. Our planet has metaphorically shrunk into a global community, with technology the magic that has made it possible. Information travels at lightning speed, and we are mostly free to mix and match ideas as we choose. Sherpas in the Himalayas covet the latest iPhone, as builders attend yoga classes in London. A concoction of instant knowledge, materialism, economics, and standardised education has led us all down the same dark alley; Western, Eastern, or otherwise.

Information shapes our thinking. Thinking shapes our world. Ideas become scribbles on beer mats, scribbles become plans, plans become foundations, and eventually our design stands tall before us, a single thought now materialised. Thoughts are as bountiful and varied as the sweets in the pick-and-mix of the Woolworths of my childhood. Both right and wrong are permitted. We are free to think whatever we choose, free to scribble some or all (or none) of them down and turn them into our latest creation. Successfully created unkind dreams equal the amount of compassionate ones just the same. Examples of both litter history.

Our thinking, then, determines the quality of our lives.

The phrases of an era give away the intentions and thoughts of its people. In the future, I wonder if we may employ "philosophical archaeologists" who no longer dig in dirt but instead examine a country's clichés, phrases, and punch lines to establish "what the hell happened to these people". More than ever in these modern times, we are encouraged to strive and to strive hard. "Climb the corporate ladder", "No pain, no gain", "Train hard, fight easy", "Stand up for yourself", "Stand out from the crowd", "Be, do, and have more"—all are ideas that portray constant striving. It is the expected norm to reach for new horizons.

Our economics, arguably the most dominant force in our lives, are built upon a concept of perpetual growth. If we are not moving forward, we are falling behind, failing. Failing feels uncomfortable, and we try to avoid discomfort at all costs. It is painful, and it causes us to suffer. We don't want it. So we push on forward to achieve more, be more, and have more in an endless battle to avoid the trauma of failing and being ostracised by the achievers (real or imagined). It is progress but with pain. This type of evolution hurts as it is being chased and yet again once it has been attained. Realisation dawns that the next level now has to be fought for too. It is an endless cycle of stress, strife, pain, and suffering. With this much hard work, is it any wonder we get headaches, depression, fatigue, obesity, cancer, diabetes, heart disease, toothache, all types of ache? The good news is that it doesn't have to be this way.

And Buddha said all this too, apparently, millennia ago somewhere in India. He taught that people had misunderstood the purpose of life:

it is not to strain on an endless cycle of impossible accomplishment, he said. The people responded that if they weren't doing "stuff", then they might as well as be dead. "'Things need to get done", they told him; "Live life to the full", they protested. Buddha understood their arguments. Yes, they could, and indeed should, lead a comprehensive and creative life – but without the stress and strain. Why not? They could do it, and he would show them how. Would they like to learn? They would, they said.

Mindfulness, then, is that lesson: the antidote to never-ending stressful striving – the need to keep up with the Joneses. When striving, our attention is always in one of two places: a past no longer available or a future yet to come. Regrets about the past fuel the fears of missing out on a better tomorrow. With all this to-ing and fro-ing between imaginary states, there is simply no time to rest in the only time we can affect: now. Mindfulness is the practice of existing in this middle time between past and future. It is a simple practice. It is not, however, an easy one.

The plethora of material about mindfulness contains detailed information on practice and training; it is a learnt skill after all. Mindful meditation, mindful walking, mindful chanting, mindful praying, mindful gardening – indeed anything can be used to practise mindfulness. My interpretation of the key concepts behind the instructions: simply do what you are doing, be quiet, pay attention and carry on doing what you are doing. That's the long and the short of it. I've read all the manuals.

Of course, the mind refuses to cooperate initially. Why would it? It's been busy thinking for so long. In mindfulness meditation, for example, just because our body is still, our to-do list halted, and our intention firmly on focusing, that doesn't mean our mind will stop churning out its endless thoughts. It continues with its habit of alternating between past and future, regret and fantasy, redirecting to everywhere other than here.

Our discerning mind separates us from animals, supposedly. We have the mental capacity to review the past and plan for our futures, all with the aim of improving our present moments. But there is a minor glitch in this latest version of human thinking – version 1.0. There is no safety measure written into our DNA coding that prevents us from remaining stuck in the past, ruminating, or needlessly worrying about tomorrow. Prolonged wading in either state comes at the expense of the one they were designed to improve, the present. Maybe upgrade 2.0 will bring improvements, whenever that may be.

When you first start mindfulness practice, of which meditation is the most common, it serves as confirmation that we are, indeed, distracted. Far from calm, centred nowness, the newly scheduled moments of quietude reveal how many billion thoughts are squeezed tightly between our ears. Frankly, it is a little depressing. Before starting practice, at least we were ignorant of our mental labyrinths. At this stage, many reject mindfulness training. It's too challenging. The cost, namely frustration, does not outweigh the gains that as yet cannot be fathomed. It is a shame – a skill vital to mental peace and happiness abandoned in its infancy.

But on the 88, mindfulness is as good as guaranteed. Why? With up to sixteen hours of walking each day, mindfulness is forced upon you, without compromise. Focusing on what you are doing and fully engaging with the task at hand is somewhat easier to when there is little else to do all day.

My first insight into mindfulness came between Temples 23, Yakuōji, and 24, Hatsumisakiji. By now I had calculated that to finish the pilgrimage, I would have to, on occasion, walk all night as well as all day. Original calculations, made on the back of a napkin served with nuts on the plane, showed that I would have to walk roughly 47 kilometres a day. This daily marathon and a half of craziness for thirty consecutive days, would allow me to complete all 1,400 kilometres of this godforsaken trip in time for my return flight to London - if I was lucky. Robert Burns, that wise old Scot, knew of the folly of trusting schedules when he wrote the oft-quoted words, "The best-laid schemes o' mice an' men/ Gang aft a-gley."

Exhaustion led to a walking pace of snail speeds, and getting lost added miles to the final distance. Stopping to chat (because it would be rude not to), stopping to heal (those boots were still killing me), stopping to help others (after all, if Buddha had a big heart then I should at least try) – all these served to knock my napkin calculations well out of bounds. A mighty six. Inevitably, night walking reared its ugly head as the only solution.

I had to steel myself for the nights that I would have to walk, for three reasons: I'm not a big fan of the dark, it's incredibly cold at night with nowhere open for food or shelter, and it would be almost 141 kilometres before my next full night's sleep. Not only is walking 141 kilometres physically demanding, it is also mentally demanding. For two days and one night, it is all you are doing, aside from small stops to rest, eat, and refresh. There is no extraneous entertainment, distraction, or social life. No cinemas, restaurants, or gyms, no music, Internet or Kindles on the 88. There is no hanging out with friends, other than those that you may meet, briefly, as they come and go while walking the same trials. Life on the 88 is life stripped down. Pilgrims have made a conscious decision to step outside the norms of society: they are walking through society – Shikoku's – but for the duration of the trip, they are not of it.

Some of the minimalism is functional; it is impossible to carry a heavy rucksack with all your worldly belongings and luxuries for over eight hundred miles. Some of it is natural. Much of the pilgrimage trails through forests, mountains, and valleys divorced from the hustle and bustle of towns and cities. Some of it is a personal choice, a decision to live free of the extremes and complexities of day-to-day living. A life lived in neon at home can be lived in pastel while a pilgrim.

With grand distraction refused and unavailable, we have the mental time and space to become witness to the multitude of thoughts that tirelessly stream through our minds. Our attention is turned instead toward the chatter in our heads, with nowhere else for it to go. Walking becomes a moving meditation. Observing thoughts, we see that they come and go of their own volition, as if being churned out on a production conveyor belt located in the deepest recesses of the mind. We also notice that they remain only if we pay them heed; reaching out and plucking a single thought from the conveyor gives it permission to come alive and reproduce. An idea picked is suddenly animated, and as with the silky threads of a spider's web, it attaches itself to another, then another, then another, each following thought needing the preceding one on which to base its existence. The bridge that connects the threads is that of choice: the choice of continued engagement in thought until it manifests as reality. A collection of new ideas, beliefs, philosophies, and concepts are formed. Eventually.

We also learn that, if left alone, thoughts evaporate with inattention. We can prevent the web from being spun. The energy source of creation has been cut off, and for now, this new network will remain undone. This understanding is critical. By watching thoughts, we realise that it is also possible to separate from them. We are free to sit in the auditorium of our mind as an observer rather than a participant. In doing so, we may comprehend that it is all just make-believe, a figment of the imagination. We choose the story. There is no predetermined script here.

Of course, we are free to choose any outcome. We are free to watch the torrent of plans, ideas, and thoughts come and go, letting them rise and fall without grasping or fuelling any of them. We are allowed to pick one, understanding that it is of our choosing, but then, once we are finished with it, are free to let it go, just as quickly. Or we can decide to get up on stage, becoming immersed in the act, believing that this thought, this make-believe, is a reality and play this part until we remember that it is all just drama. Many are choosing drama, to become lost in parts of their own choosing. To make advances, first we must recognise and accept where we are so that we can decide where it is we would rather be.

And so it was, on that day between Temples 23 and 24, with the salty sea mist blowing in off the Pacific Ocean, that I would fully face my mind's noise. I would stand in front of it, saturated with all the buzz and complexity, and see once and for all its importance in my life. The sun was getting heavy and dropping for the day. Evening cool was reaching inside my clothes. The day-night-day walk was coming to an end, and I would rest tonight, shattered. Thousands of steps of walking had created a hypnotic rhythm that had helped suspend all thinking, planning, considering, and pondering. A beautiful but simple scenery offered little distraction, and exhaustion prevented motivation to create any. I had nowhere left to be but with the next step of the next mile of this closing day.

And suddenly there I was, just being, totally aware of my surroundings and myself, with thoughts coming, going, and then slowing to a halt. I existed in a seemingly wide-open space filled with potential but free from the restrictions of thought. I was content merely resting in that moment. It was perfect. I felt no desire to compare it to anything from the past or hope for its maintenance in the future, I was just fully immersed in its immediacy.

The present had an unmistakable power and presence. It felt as I imagine Mount Everest feels, if it could, allowing the weathers to come and go around its peaks: Looking on. Letting it all just be. Not needing to get involved. Happy existing. Standing dominant. More than the joy that came with the relief of imminent rest was the joy that came with the profound peace that came with just leaving thoughts alone. No straining. No changing. No analysing. No fixing. I had walked into mindfulness. And it was good.

But in that profound and peaceful silence, something else was revealed.

CHAPTER 8

"Universe Requesting"

Create we must.
It is the way that life smiles.
Making.
Evolving.
—*Journal entry*

Istood immersed in that profound and penetrating calm. Few thoughts remained to disturb it; those that from time to time did pop up faded quickly without attention to anchor them. I felt like the white of an untouched canvas; potential before being realised. Was this how the big bang felt moments before banging? From here, I felt I could have chosen any outcome. I could decide to paint in greens or reds, light strokes or thick, pastels, acrylic, ink or pencil, landscape, portrait, animal or man; or nothing, or later.

At that moment, I discovered the answer to an inevitable question that arises out of meditation practice: Where do the thoughts come from that we are attempting to calm? Now I knew. Here I was standing at the birthplace of thoughts, words, scribbles, plans, and creation – standing at the gateway of life.

I know these are bold statements. Some may accuse me of rehashing Buddhist concepts in an attempt to make sense of my experience. They may be right, but I feel satisfied, then and now, that I was directly experiencing life's pure potential. It was unquestionable to me. Have you ever been so confident that you just knew something was right, even though you probably couldn't explain why? With this type of certainty, we don't even need to explain why, to others or ourselves. We don't mind the doubters. They don't matter on this occasion.

These blissful states are fleeting at first. Maybe each subsequent experience gets longer, deeper, and more profound. Whatever the duration, they still provide flashes of insight into the workings and mysteries of the mind and, in turn, of life.

Words jabbed at my peripheries, and I was moved to write this into my journal:

> Create we must.
> It is the way that life smiles.
> Making.
> Evolving.

With distraction temporarily calmed, I think I was witness to the essence that sits behind all life; the substance upon which all else builds its foundations. It was here all along; how could it not be? I had just been too busy to look as deeply into its eyes before.

It's easy for this to happen. How often are we distracted from the love that is present in our lives? Like the fleeting peck on your partner's cheek as you pass from the front door to the computer to check emails just moments after arriving home; half-hearted efforts playing with the children – token gestures – before taking that important phone call as they look on, bewildered, at the absent parent in their midst; a rushed walk around the block with the dog, to be back in time for your favourite programme – all the joy of a pet's unconditional companionship traded for a half-hour soap opera. Be careful holding back attention from the loves in your life. They may not always be content with your distraction, and they may one day walk away unnoticed, while you bury your head in your smartphone. Not so smart.

It's all right. We all make these mistakes. We are all, to some extent, taking those we love for granted. Life is a work in progress, after all. Sometimes the paintings with which we fill our canvas are not as beautiful as planned, once we step back and review, but we can start again, anytime. Creation is our birthright. It is how life expresses itself, through us expressing ourselves. We have the right to choose whatever outcome we desire. It is, in fact, our duty as recipients of life. The choices we make help the blank canvas live, sing, and animate. Our choices give life to life itself. I call this process "Universe Requesting".

The clearer we are about what we want, the more easily and quickly it will become manifest. Imagine standing at your easel, brush in hand, ready to paint a horse. You begin but then become distracted by a dog barking outside. "Now," you think, "I'd like to draw a dog." You change colours and begin your new creation; you'll come back to the horse another time. You continue working on your dog. Excellent. Until the doorbell rings and the mail carrier hands you a parcel with the book of birds you ordered. You have a break for tea, flip through the beautiful illustrations, and now you'd like to paint a hummingbird.

You can see where this is going. It doesn't take much to realise that fractured efforts slow progress, and concentrated efforts accelerate it. Life is waiting, urging to be realised, but it would appreciate some clarity. "Thy will be done," said the Lord – "a bit quicker, if you stop changing your mind", he might well have added!

I was clear on the theory, but it was time to experiment with the practicalities, both for fun and to prove their validity. Let the games begin. Strawberry cake. That's what I chose to create first.

I was in the middle of a bamboo grove miles from anywhere somewhere in Kochi Prefecture. Shikoku is an island divided into four prefectures (like our counties, but bigger): Tokushima, Kochi, Ehime, and Kagawa. Although part of the same island, each has a distinct essence, topography, and flavour. I had stopped in a *kyūkeishō* to eat my lunch. A *kyūkeishō* is a small hut, usually wooden, for pilgrims to shelter and rest. They are open sided like a tree house from childhoods gone by (only not in the trees) and not designed for overnight sleeping. I loved finding a *kyūkeishō*. It felt as if I'd found a great hideaway, and you never knew where you would find one. They are marked on Japanese pilgrim maps, but I didn't have one; besides, the maps are nearly unfathomable and mostly incorrect. So the joy of stumbling across the wooden shelters remained.

Bamboo surrounded me, its dusty blue, out of the corner of my eye, turning green when I looked closer. The colour never fails to calm me. Bamboo has a slight cracking and creaking sound too, as it bends in the breeze. I love this natural percussion. It is music to my ears. Well fed, stupidly calm and lying on my back with a slice of the sun warming my body, I decided upon strawberry cake for dessert. I'm not a massive fan of strawberry cake. It just seemed like a highly unlikely thing to find miles from anywhere while on pilgrimage in the middle of Japan. If I was going to test theories about "Universe Requesting", then why not start with a British sounding dessert? At least it was a demand in tune with other food-based miracles of the past (bread and fish orders in Galilee).

"I'd like strawberry cake, please. Thank you."

That's how I order when I'm "Universe Requesting". Then I try to go about my day and forget about it. The forgetting part is much harder than it sounds. More often than not, deep-rooted doubts call from the abyss: "This won't work", "Miracles are make-believe", "Be realistic", "Grow up."

I packed my lunch things and hoisted my rucksack onto my back. I still had many miles to cover today, and the hills and bamboo groves were a beautiful but challenging terrain. On the uneven surfaces of the countryside, twisting an ankle is always a real possibility.

I had hadn't seen many buildings all day – not any, in fact – and my view ahead didn't suggest any lay ahead. Today was a day of walking out in the back of beyond. Suddenly, but unannounced and unexpected suddenly, the trees and bamboo thinned, and I found myself on a little road into a tiny town. The first building I came to was a shop with a yellow roof. I distinctly remember that yellow roof, the colour and shade vividly imprinted on my mind.

I couldn't read the sign outside; the *kanji* was too advanced for my painfully limited Japanese vocabulary. So I looked in the window to see what they sold. Not much. It looked as if they were coming to the end of their day, for the window was sparse. But there, displayed on a solitary plastic stand, was a single slice of cheesecake with a strawberry topping!

"Oh!" I thought. I think I said it out loud, involuntarily. I bought the strawberry cake, ate it, and walked on.

The pendulum swing between faith and doubt is a curious thing. We gain insights throughout our lives that we instinctively know to be true. They often change the course of our thinking, behaviour, and ultimately our lives. I had one of these when I stumbled across "Universe Requesting" in action. I hadn't doubted it until I saw it working.

What is this perverse side of human nature that questions and tries either to trivialise or justify something that is plainly true and magical? Do we not want to believe we are creating our worlds by our choices? Do we dare not admit that it is we who create our paths? It was not the first time I had faced my doubting Thomas.

For several summers, years ago during my tennis coaching days, I was flown out to Germany to teach tennis, martial arts, and meditation to a wealthy and influential Bavarian family. Every year their infamous summer soirée attracted celebrities and royalty from around the world. It was crazy and eye opening for a twenty-four-year-old father of one, with another not far off.

As a guest, I was given the family's own private hunting lodge to stay in – a wooden eight-bedroom Bavarian house filled with more memories forgotten, than I had yet had. Other guests shared rooms and floors in the main house up the hill. Between the lodge and the main house was a three-hundred-metre walk up the drive. Halfway along was a pen of goats, I think destined for the soirée menu. I said good morning to them every day, while they ignored me and continued to chomp grass. I didn't reach in to pet them because of the sign that said: "BEWARE-ELECTRIC FENCE." One morning, I wondered if the fence shocked humans in the same way as goats. I just can't help this sort of curiosity, it seems. The kick that shot up my arm and clicked my jaw proved that yes, the electric voltage worked on humans too. No doubts about that at all. It was probably why the sign was there.

The next day, I started to question the experience. I know, I can hear you. What an idiot, right? But my doubting Thomas was wondering if I was now immune to the massive electric shock.

No. I think it made me lose a couple of breaths the second time around, a bit as though someone had served a tennis ball at my chest. Hard. All the goats carried on chomping. However, one goat bothered to lift its gaze, if not its head, with a look that could not be confused with anything but contempt: "Idiot", I think I heard it bleat. I'd like to admit that this is the end of the story. Sadly I cannot. I'm duty bound to tell the truth and demonstrate the perverse nature of doubt.

The next day my doubt had managed to assume Godzilla proportions. I now wondered if maybe my technique was wrong. If I held on tighter, could I outgrip the electricity in the fence? I had to go back to my room for a little lie down afterwards and change my tracksuit bottoms, which were covered in grass stains from where I'd landed in the bushes ten feet away from the goat pen. I never said good morning to the goats again. I also wondered if I should have persisted with the sports psychologist all those years ago. This was a prime example of the kind of doubt that had continued throughout my pilgrimage in Japan.

It seems as if we fear to put our faith in the concept of "Ask and it is given". We worry that reality might shatter our hopes and hearts when it confirms that the idea is untrue. We don't want to discover that life isn't abundant after all. We don't want to know our lives are governed not by us and that there is no real choice in the matter. The fall from hope to despair is further than the drop from despair to ground zero. I can see why people refuse to believe in the positive; many have had lives that confirm, to them anyway, that life is neither abundant nor fair nor kind. It would be gratuitous to play devil's advocate and wonder if they might have chosen a better outcome. Certainly we risk big falls when we aim and miss, but we also risk missing out on life's splendour by failing to dream big. In a way, by walking to prove that time and money were just obstacles of our choosing, I could also show that life wants us to paint the most fantastic vistas for ourselves. Or not. It is our choice, ultimately; free will and all that.

The only way I could prove that my strawberry cake was not a coincidence was to do it again. Manifest something else. I wondered what I could conjure up next.

If I walk for any length of time with a backpack, I get a sharp pain on a high point of my right shoulder blade. Sometimes it makes my arm go numb; other times it gives me a fuzzy headache. It has been a problem for years. On the 88 the pain was horrific and a definite contender for some serious "Universe Requesting" action. The request was "Dear Universe, please help fix this pain. Thank you. *Dōmo arigatō gozaimasu.*" I always added a thank-you in Japanese. I was in Japan after all, and it seemed the polite thing to do. I don't know if God changes race, colour, or creed depending on country of operation. Who knows?

Request made, I carried on with my day's walking.

I have no idea how much later – maybe an hour, maybe twenty minutes, maybe two hours – but when I stretched my arm away from my side to relieve some of the pain building up in my scapula, I felt a whoosh of warmth from the pain point of my shoulder, down the full length of my arm and fingers and then, as I imagined, out and away from my body. And that was that. I didn't have the pain anymore. Gone. It never returned while I was in Japan. Once again, doubts started to work immediately over this second mini-miracle. "It was the stretch that did it", said the voices, "the movement of walking released the knot", they jeered, but my belief in what had happened was growing. Although still present, the doubts were subsiding as confidence in "Universe Requesting" gathered momentum.

I played this game all day: I asked for food, toilets, and company; to see a yellow car and a bus; to find a restaurant within the next hundred yards, a park in three hundred steps, and a bowl of spaghetti carbonara before sunset. I got it all. Everything. I had to stop requesting because I started to freak myself out. It was clear that whatever I asked for, I was given. With this experience came both excitement at the potential but also trepidation at the responsibility of such a realisation. Knowing that we are responsible for our choices is a daunting prospect. We only have ourselves to blame

CHAPTER 9

Letting Go

Trust means to let go.
—Journal entry

AND THEN IT stopped working. The "Universe Requesting" just stopped working as it had been.

I was deep in Ehime Prefecture, the third of the island's four regions and well over halfway through the pilgrimage. It had been another long, hard day's walking, and my mood was starting to shift for the worse. The day before I had been buoyed by experiments with "Universe Requesting" and felt lighter through finally having an insight into how life works. Or so I thought. Without any cause or reason that I was aware of, I began to feel antsy. Every thought was spiky. I felt flat; each step was more effort than I could be bothered making. My peripheries were dark even though the sun was shining. Sunlight didn't gently warm my face today; it stung my eyes and burnt my skin.

I figured that I needed rest, to bring this day to an end and sleep it off, suspecting a pilgrim's hangover – that state of physical, emotional, and spiritual despondency known to strike walkers of the 88 from time to time. So looking skyward, I requested that I soon come across a place to stop for the night. Shortly, I met a local man who told me that, not more than twenty minutes ahead, there was a place to rest, and he gave me a map to help me find it. Thank God. Two and a half hours later though, I was no longer thanking God, the man, or "Universe Requesting".

I think the Japanese like puzzles; they must do. It's why they suffocate airport newsagents with volumes of sudoku and why they design their maps so that foreigners like me can't decipher the damn things! I binned the map, chewed the inside of my lip so hard that it bled, and had a killer headache from all the aggression and tension held taut in my neck and shoulders. I was not a happy man, and sitting down by the side of the road, I raged.

I raged about maps, people who give poor directions and the tiredness in my legs. I raged about the boots that were rubbing my ankles raw, the trousers that were so hot they made my knees itch, and the scratching of my unshaven beard. I raged about past regrets, missed opportunities, and moments of cowardice. And I raged about "Universe Requesting" and why it had suddenly forsaken me. I raged until the anger tried to leave me as tears. My shoulders shook as I sobbed, a reaction utterly out of proportion to the problem at hand, but I didn't care. I was too tired for rational thought. I felt lonely, abandoned, exhausted, and broken, mentally, physically, and spiritually. I had nothing left and lay down, rucksack still on my back, and closed my eyes to the world.

Suddenly I was forced to jump up out of the way as a small beaten up Nissan Micra came hurtling around the blind bend, almost crushing my feet. Could today get any worse? The car screeched to a halt a little further on, once its ageing brakes had finally managed to work up the energy to effect a stop (Hello, has anyone heard of an MOT test?).

A bald little head popped out of the passenger window. "You need a place to stay?" he called.

"Er, yes,"

"Get in. We take you."

I explained that I was walking the 88, and thank you, but I needed to walk the whole way.

"Ah yes, of course. Splendid."

It was then that I noticed that not only was he wearing the unmistakable robes of a Buddhist monk, but so were the other three smiling heads crammed into the mini motor.

"You keep going. One hundred metres straight on this

road – *masugu* – straight." And with that, they drove off waving and smiling. I had almost been killed, and then saved, by four monks in a Micra. I wrote that down in my journal. You can't make this stuff up! Just as the monk had said, I arrived at the rest stop minutes later. It was like none I had come across so far.

Almost all of the temporary rest spots for the 88's pilgrims had so far been fairly uniform in design and upkeep. They looked as if local councils had grudgingly catered for the needs of pilgrims only on the insistence of residents' pressure and the council's subsequent fear of lost votes. Budget-driven shelter was erected with all the character, care, and exuberance that local councils know how to deliver. At least now the locals were assuaged, and maybe Buddha too. Yet this new place was different.

I saw it just over the small hill after the bridge. It appeared to be built of salvaged wood. Makeshift annexes had been added to meet demand; haphazard add-ons that told an evolving story of pilgrim shelter. This place felt like somewhere trying to gift thanks to pilgrims for their efforts and sacrifice while on the 88. It had places to sleep, a bathroom, and units to prepare food or unpack convenience meals bought on the road. There were even more places to sleep – demand must be high for this eccentric haven. Additionally provided was a central lounge where a fire burned at night and where guests told stories about their lives and experiences. This creaky old place felt like a commune rather than a temporary shelter.

It was here that I met the three stooges - Hear-No-Evil, See-No-Evil and Speak-No-Evil. The stooges were sitting around the fire. I stumbled in with my backpack and introduced myself. They smiled from where they sat, and Hear-No-Evil stood up to show me where to put my bag and where I could sleep and then asked if I was hungry. He wasn't tall, but he was huge in presence. He had the flat, square nose of a seasoned fighter and mangled cauliflower ears that made me wonder when he had last heard anything with clarity. A powerful back and shoulders tested the seams of the tweed blazer he was wearing. The jacket looked as if it had come from one of those plastic bags people leave outside charity shops when they can't be bothered to wait for opening time to donate.

"Onaka ga akimashita ka?"

I answered that I was, indeed, hungry. Hear-No-Evil brought me a box meal from a fridge tucked away in a dim corner. It's hard to pinpoint exactly why this was the most delicious meal I have ever had. Maybe it was because I was simply famished and was at last fed. Maybe it was because the gift of kindness that comes with such an offering touches the heart deeply. Maybe it was because my earlier despair at the failing process of "Universe Requesting" had been replaced by relief that it hadn't failed me at all. Whatever the reason, it was delicious.

I sat around the fire with them, eating, enjoying the warmth, and feeling calmed by the flickering flames and the dancing shadows on the walls of this crazy, wonderful place. They chatted gently amongst themselves as I ate, and the tones of their voices comforted me. I felt at home, and it made me teary and emotional. Well fed and relaxed, I watched the stooges through tired eyes. They reminded me of untold deities that appear throughout the Buddhist tradition.

Buddhism doesn't have a single central god who runs the show. It has many different characters, mostly representing states of the mind. *Nyorai*: enlightened beings – Buddhas – hold the highest position in a hierarchy of holiness. Bodhisattvas, while training under the *Nyorai*, do their very best to save all people from ignorance. *Myōō*: are gods serving as messengers to the *Nyorai*; and Devas (not the prom queen type) and heavenly kings borrowed from the Brahmin tradition to which Buddhism is inextricably linked.

Confused? I am, too. I have been reading and learning about these characters for years now and still have no clear understating of what the differences are. I can only conclude that the diversity of religious characters and symbols has evolved to represent every challenge, dilemma, and circumstance that human devotees may encounter. "I'm struggling with a migraine", Takako tells her friend; "Go and worship *Yakushi Nyorai*; he is the Buddha of sickness and healing" might be the advice. "I'm travelling soon. Any suggestions?" "Travel insurance and *Jizō Bosatsu*" may be the reply. "I feel I need protecting from all four evil directions. Can you help?" "We've got you covered; check out the four heavenly kings – they'll see you right!" comes the response.

Eventually, See-No-Evil spoke and interrupted my daydreams. He asked me about my trip so far and my background. I told him about my love of the martial arts, the Japanese arts in particular, and he beamed a wide, toothless smile. I wasn't sure why until later, when Hear-No-Evil told me things about See-No-Evil that he was too humble say himself.

See-No-Evil was born blind to a family of swordsmiths. The family had been producers of the famous razor-sharp Japanese long sword, the katana, for generations. He had shown such a talent for the art of sword making that at one stage in his career, he had made *katana* for the emperor of Japan. He was a legend in his field. And now, here he was sitting around a fire in a shack for pilgrims with me, a foreigner, his two friends, and piles of empty crushed beer cans. I wondered how this came to be.

The three stooges, like Hajime-san before, were homeless. They lived outside of the day-to-day routines of the "nine to fivers", existing frugally and whiling away their time. They all liked a drink. Hajime-san had told me: "It keeps out the cold, Mattō-san." Much of their time now was spent helping those walking the 88 temple pilgrimage. Did this make the stooges its guardians? Why did they choose to do it? How long had they done it? How long would they continue to do it? Where were their families? Had they ever walked the 88 themselves?

My questions remained unasked and unanswered; they slipped away as I fell asleep surrounded by the dark amber of the flickering flames and the occasional crack of burning wood. I dreamt all night of Buddhas, gods, and guardians and woke in the morning feeling calm and happy. I was ready for another day on the road and was grateful for the salvation of this place.

As I continued on the 88, the three Stooges now behind me but still in my heart and mind, my experiences so far rattled around inside trying, I guess, to organise themselves into hypotheses that I could understand and utilise. I thought further about my experiences with "Universe Requesting", both its successes and failures, and I had some flashes of insight. Important pieces of the puzzle that I hadn't understood as clearly before fell into place. Maybe the relaxing evening at the commune had paved the way for this new comprehension. Maybe the three stooges, somehow, had brought me clarity.

I considered the art of letting go. And it is an art, something that requires practice and what my friend and karate mentor, Kris, calls "feathering the accelerator". Buddhists teach that grasping is a root of suffering. Its opposite, letting go, alleviates it.

But what does the concept of grasping look like in our daily lives? When we are out walking the dog in the park and stop to admire and smell a beautiful flower, then pick it to take home to our partner where it withers and dies in a vase. When we take our son or daughter to a stadium hosting a sporting final and watch most of the match through our smartphone lens so that we can post our experience on social media, our eyes missing that all-important goal. When we visit a natural wonder and ignore the wind on our cheeks as we busily adjust the filter and colour on that amazing "money shot" we just took. When we look on in awe at the few wild animals still roaming freely on our planet and then rush into the gift shop to buy a bracelet of its hair to wear, not realising that this is just another degree of "trophy hunting". These are all examples of grasping that we have all indulged in to some degree. It is an inability to live an experience and then walk away from it, merely grateful for the moment that has now passed. Why do we do this? Why do we feel the need to own and control experiences that have gone?

As I walked, I wondered if our habitual grasping is born of fear and mistrust. For instance, if you knew that you were guaranteed the smell of another beautiful bloom, you wouldn't need to pick the first. If you understood that life's unseen organising was working behind the scenes on your behalf, it would be unnecessary to take on the impossible task of controlling events. If you understood that good times follow bad, each and every time, would you still need to cling tight to moments of happiness? No. They'll be back.

There is of course an inherent paradox here: the contradiction of simultaneously desiring something and letting go of it. This is where Kris's phrase, "feathering the accelerator", comes to good use. It is an art of subtle balancing. Certainly we must desire something enough to want to bother grabbing and preserving it, yet we must also let go and trust the heavens to deliver without interference. Our well-meaning but futile interjections have consequences otherwise.

Consider the following: At a restaurant, when you order a meal, it will be served, you trust. Unless you have stumbled into a café carpeted with goat faeces, high up an Andean mountain ridge, you just know you'll get your meal. It may come soon or a little later, but you believe it will come, and you are free to continue a conversation with your dinner date without wasting further thought on your order. Trust (in the restaurant) has allowed you to let go of the desire (the order) until it is ready to be enjoyed (served). Goal achieved. It's a simple example, I know, but it is the same process involved in all creation, whether starting a family, building a career, climbing Everest, or ordering pizza. That confidence in the process, of course, has come initially from positive experiences in the past: you ordered, they served, you trust, and the cycle perpetuates. We have seen, and so we now believe.

But what of situations where we have little or no prior experience? No previous track record on which to build confidence. Let's return to our Andean café. We sit down and look around. It's like nowhere we've ever eaten before; a stone building with a few battered wooden tables and chairs. No music, just the sound of goats bleating and the clank of pots and pans, from what must be the kitchen. An unshaven old man takes our order – goat curry, of course – and we watch him shuffle away.

We know little about this place, and doubt creeps in. Why is no one eating here? Is it clean? Will we get salmonella? Can you even get salmonella from goat curry? Why is it taking so long? Shall we ask? Shall I ask? Can you ask? Let's not ask? We really should, right? So we ask. We head toward the kitchen and tap lightly on the door.

"Sí, Señor, how can I help you?" asks the unshaven old man poking his head from behind the kitchen door

"Erm, hi, yes, I was just wondering if everything is OK with our order?"

"Sí, Señor, yes, please take a seat."

So we sit down again and wait, and wait and wait. "Hello, hello, excuse me, hello", we ask a little louder, the second time around.

"It's coming, Señor, please take *a seat.*" A little stronger too, as the old man realises that he has a back seat driver in his midst.

On our third inquiry, the little old man asks us to leave. We have offended him, his family, and his restaurant by interfering. Embarrassed, we go sheepishly, leaving the goat café behind. Later we find out that the goat curry is so good that people come from all over, just to have it. The café was empty because it was a public holiday, and the little old man only opened for us. We looked tired and hungry as we came up the hill. We looked as if we could do with his famous goat curry, but it would take a little time today: he was on his own, as the rest of the kitchen staff was away enjoying the day off.

Doubt and uncertainty encourage us to make assumptions that are rarely correct. We then hold on to these make-believes like a dog that won't let go of its bone. A false assumption often brings poor choices and almost always injures a situation. Contrary imaginings rarely help the creative process. Attempting to control the unknown is always ultimately pointless.

My first run-in with futile control tactics was as a tennis player during tennis tournaments. Occasionally I would stumble upon that rare blend of relaxed alertness that would lead to playing fantastically well – even if I do say so myself. On one occasion I played four service games in a row without losing a point. If I wasn't hitting aces, I was hitting unreturnable serves. I just couldn't miss the target. As I led by a set and a half in the quarter-final of a county championship, at change of ends my opponent complimented me: "Wow, man, I can't get near your serve today. What are you doing?"

I smiled vaingloriously, but the damage had been done. Up until then, I hadn't even thought about my serve. I was just doing it. Fully immersed in the process, I was merely serving bombs. I was calm, centred, relaxed, and happy. But then I started to think. I thought about the action, the ball toss, the rhythm, the grip on my racquet, all in an attempt to understand the magic, grasp it, and keep it coming. I didn't hit another ball in court from that moment. Trying hard to serve well, I served a double fault. With each double fault, I tried harder to control my action; to duplicate the past, and serve out the set. With each failure,

I strained harder to manipulate the future. I knew what I wanted to do and was determined to get it done, but to no avail. I lost the match.

This type of single-mindedness, this extreme and panic-ridden need to control circumstance can disrupt the creative process, both in accuracy and speed of success. It is something familiar to many of us. The human mind is a double-edged blade. Focused, committed, and effortless use of our cognitive powers allows us to create, almost literally, heaven on earth; the same mind using doubt, assumption, tension, and control is equally able to light the flames of hell under our feet. History and today's news reports show us that we are yet to use our faculties as tools to guarantee a better today. Instead, our immature minds tend toward rumination, daydream, and doubt. We are stuck in places that don't exist: past and future. The beautiful present is a gift often ignored.

Ironically it is often pain, fear, and doubt in the extreme that finally allow us to let go and lead us to our original goal. By the side of the road, as I desired rest and comfort, head in hands and distraught, my tears helped me reach the place of "Damn it, I give up." At that moment, obsessive striving now released, my desire appeared unimpeded, just around the next bend. Yet what a painful process, and I'm not certain it needs to be this way. I've given this much thought, both on and off the 88, and am unconvinced that pain needs to proceed happiness. We don't need to pay some holy penance before joy is allowed. I just don't think that the human mind, version 1.0, has yet fathomed how to master joy without hardship. Maybe the upgrade to version 2.0 will include this improvement and fix the bug. Maybe it's about the goals we set, the questions we ask, and the orders we make. Maybe we just need to choose better. Maybe we could pick anything we like, but remember to add the postscript: "Oh, by the way, may I have this without the side order of hassle, please?"

That's what I did for the rest of the pilgrimage. I started to make my requests and trust that they were on their way. Sometimes it was easier to imagine than at other times. Doubts remained, as I practised the art of trusting and letting go. So when the trust wasn't free flowing, I distracted myself from the questions, false assumptions and attempts to regain control. Sometimes I just pretended that I had trust in the process — "Fake it till you make it", to use a team building cliché. Other times when physical tension had built up through my mistrust, I relaxed it with stretches and calisthenics; all of these techniques aimed at "feathering the accelerator" of trust and letting go. With every success it became easier, and I became a little calmer.

Other thoughts came to me that morning. I remembered a conversation with God. Neale Donald Walsch, author of *Conversations with God*, explains the failures of "Universe Requesting" in another way. I include it here, in my own words, as another important consideration for when life is not looking as you would like. He says that for something to come into being (a holiday, money, love, health, anything), its opposite must appear beforehand. It sounds a little counterintuitive, I know, but turn your mind back to the yin-yang symbol that I mentioned earlier: black contains white, as white contains black. Each needs the contrast of the other to exist. If I walked into a room full of "me" – short, bald, bushy eyebrows, and a broken nose – how would I know who "me" is? Everyone there would be short and bald with bushy eyebrows and a broken nose. I could only know "me" if something other than "me" came into the room to act as a contrast; let's say Burt – tall, blond, and athletic. Contrast is how we understand and get to know ourselves, and Walsch teaches that at the moment that you "Universe Request" something, its opposite is born. It's an idea at least worth considering.

It had been a busy morning of insight. The day before I was on the brink of despair, today I was shining with hope and clarity. The 88 certainly offered a roller coaster of mental states. The last thing I remember about that day was someone once telling me that they fully believed that life is actually on our side. I think I agree. Whether we choose to stress and strain or to flow and grow, ultimately life is rooting for us. It has a vested interest, after all. Does it not?

CHAPTER 10

Expect the unexpected. Always.

Expect the Unexpected

Trying to fathom the paths of synchronicity is a futile task.
Leave it to the Gods and trust in their wisdom.
—Journal entry

UNEXPECTED DIVERSIONS ON the way to our goals can be disconcerting. However, I had experienced enough of them on the 88 to begin to consider that maybe a divine order was involved. As I walked from temple to temple, life was performing magic of which I was totally unaware, but I was beginning to trust it. By the last third of the pilgrimage, I had grown to believe that the universe was on my side. I had let go of controlling the impossible, all that needed to be orchestrated to finish the 88 on time and within budget. There was no way I could manipulate the outcome. I would have to leave it to intelligent design far greater than mine.

This divine intelligence is with us all always, but as with an iceberg summiting above water, it is natural to overlook what you cannot see; the foundations beneath. Did you know that the liver is always performing any of around five hundred functions? Nerve impulses travel to and from the brain at speeds of up to two hundred fifty miles per hour. When you blush, so does the lining of your stomach. Our brain can read up to a thousand words per minute. An adult male is made up of approximately 7 octillion atoms (there are only a mere 300 billion stars in the galaxy, by the way.)

My point? Life, the universe, God, or whatever you want to

call it – it's got this. It can handle the job. It can cross the finish the line without your help, but thank you for offering. Of course, you are welcome to seek to interfere; welcome to try fathoming the synchronicities involved in life's beautiful cauldron of creation. But it's unlikely that you'll succeed, and you'll only get tired trying.

Life is going to do its thing with or without us. Our efforts to discover its secrets and own them as our own are futile. It's best just to let it be and enjoy. Life has its unique rhythms and ways. I used to try to work out how it all fits together. My human DNA is encoded to own and control circumstance just as much as the next guy's; I'm not immune. I brought this obsession with me to the 88, firmly intact. However, with each step and each experience along the way, I started to trust in life's methods; I believed in its ability to deliver the goods. But it threw curveballs at me nevertheless.

Late into the pilgrimage, when every extra mile walked and minute lost diverted me further from my goal, I set out very early one morning to pack in the mileage. Frost covered pavements, and a smoke spiral ascended from the chimney of a house that stood alone in a field. It was just before daybreak, the time when life is teetering to commence, but it is still possible to steal some of the solitary silence that is, for now, unbroken. This time of day is one of my favourites; the other, as the day descends into early evening.

Traditionally, this time of the morning is when Buddhist monks meditate. Not only does this mindfulness practice set a positive tone for the forthcoming day, but it also teaches discipline, overcoming the urge to stay in bed and instead doing something more worthwhile. But there is another thing about this time of day, and although indefinable, it is no less tangible. These moments are pregnant with spiritual power, and this is not as esoteric a concept as it first seems. Have you ever exercised at this time and felt wonderful for the rest of the day? Have you ever captured your most creative thoughts in the greys of predawn while the others in the house are still in their beds? Have you ever broken through a previously impenetrable problem with solutions offered in these powerful minutes? You know what I'm talking about if you have had just one of these experiences.

With a feeling that this was going to be a remarkable day, I set off walking. I felt energetic, inspired, and confident. I watched the day start to unfold around me as lights in houses came on and car engines started up in driveways before heading off to work. By now the sky was pink in anticipation of dawn. It was a picture postcard scene. It was a perfect moment.

I had been walking with a sense of pleasant calm for some time, just confident to hand myself over to the rhythm of the day and collect mile after mile on my journey to the end. When the sun was high enough in the sky to make it necessary to take off first my jacket and then my jumper, I was suddenly suspicious that I hadn't yet reached the next temple, as I thought by now I should have. Concern gave way to ensuing panic as I looked for somewhere or someone who could point me in the right direction. It was still early, and local shops were still some time from opening their doors to customers. Panic turned to anger with the realisation that I might have wasted hours of walking – time and energy I could ill afford to lose. This picture-perfect morning was quickly peeling at the edges.

In a narrow road flanked on both sides by a small row of shops, I saw a man arrive at his greengrocery shop. He ducked in under the half-lifted shutters to make tea before setting his stalls for the day. I pounced on the poor man. Bleary-eyed, he listened to me as I spouted my predicament at him. I'm sure I was the last thing he needed before a long day at work. He booted up his computer to see if he could find directions to the next temple and get me out of his hair. Finally, the old laptop whirred into action, but the Internet connection was down. This morning was moving from bad to worse.

It was then that the greengrocer's mother shuffled out from somewhere at the back of the shop. The curves of age hunched her, and the lines of her face told of a long, maybe hard life. It was the kindest face that I had ever seen, and she looked directly into my eyes and assured me that all would be well. First she made me sit down; then she brought us all tea. We all tucked into a packet of biscuits she took from the shelves, while the greengrocer reconnected the Internet and printed off directions for me. As he ran back and forth between the printer and the laptop, his mother asked me questions about my life and my time walking the 88. She had a mother's care.

Soon it was time to get back on my way. I bowed deeply to the greengrocer and apologised for my intrusion. Still a little bleary-eyed and shell-shocked, he laughed and wished me luck: *"Gambatte"*, he said. His mother took my hand and walked outside with me. She made certain that I had all the map printouts and gave me two more packets of biscuits to take on the journey. She gave me a huge motherly hug and stood in the middle of the road waving as I walked away.

Her kindness made me cry. It had been many years since I had felt such unconditional compassion, and this experience rattled an emotional stoicism that had chained me for many years. Maybe the barricade of goal-driven independence, the nigh on narcissistic focus that high-level sports demand, was being dismantled, brick by brick. I had unwittingly walked for more than three hours in the wrong direction, but it had led me somewhere much better.

Sometimes the diversions helped heal emotions, at other times they fed hunger or assuaged a literal thirst, and sometimes they took me around a corner where life stood waiting to show off its grandeur in a plumage of spectacular colour. One particular display that I remember was at one of the dramatic headlands of Kochi Prefecture.

It had been yet another long day on the road. I had expected to find somewhere very cheap to sleep for the night – a youth hostel, YMCA, or *tsūyadō* perhaps. It wasn't to be; a familiar story. Spotting a laundromat, I thought at least I could clean my clothes which, by this stage, were in need of some attention. I stripped down, put my clothes in the machine, covered myself with my jacket, and watched the clothes tumble. The laundromat manager sat down next to me, and we started to chat. By the time my machine had stopped whirring, it was dark outside, and the manager needed to close for the day. He tossed me the keys to the front door and asked me to lock up and post them back through the letter box when I left; he had spares. He dropped a handful of coins into my palm so that I could activate the tumble dryer and sit against it to keep myself warm, and from a cupboard he bought out a laundry basket of lost but clean property that he had rescued from the machines over the years. I made a makeshift bed with some of the clothes, and wore everything else, slotted the coins into the tumble dryer, and fell asleep, upright, against the warmth. An unexpected refuge against what turned out to be a freezing night.

The light through the laundromat window woke me early the next morning. I tidied up my temporary room and headed out onto the road. Such a sunrise such as I've never seen before or since welcomed me. I bathed for a moment in both its beauty and its gentle warmth, allowing it to inspire the beginning of a new day, grateful for the prize of the unexpected diversion.

The road never seems to travel directly from A to Z, that is clear, but despite the detours and the unexpected treats, we always seem to get to where we need to be. Or better. The alternative routes never seem to be in conflict with our original plans. They remain within the context of the primary goal, just variations on it. It is highly unlikely that a detour on the road to becoming a space traveller would redirect to the highway that leads to ornithology or artist; Broadway dancer to salsa teacher is a much more likely diversion. Why the need then, for detours? I pondered on my experience.

My childhood dream of becoming a professional tennis star was cut unceremoniously short by my lack of talent to be one. At the entry levels to professional tennis, on what is called the Satellite Tour, no crowds are waiting for your autograph. No media want to report on your off-court antics, no tennis concierge is waiting to carry your racket bag, and, more important, there is no money to speak of. Agents and sponsors are hardly falling over themselves courtside to offer you a fantastic sponsorship deal. The prize money in the lower leagues, even if you win, is never enough to cover flights and accommodation to the global events. I'm not moaning, and I'm not bitter. I fully understand that pro sports is a business, and you must earn your stripes with high-level wins before you are valuable enough to gain riches. That's how it is.

So you must find other ways to fund your dreams. I chose to teach the sport I love, in between travel, tournaments, and training, and soon came to realise that I loved the art of pedagogy much more than I loved competing. I would never have discovered my passion for teaching had I not been forced to teach to cover the expenses of competition. It was ironic that the moment I had earned enough money to afford a year of undistracted full-time competitive tournament play, I didn't want it anymore. I wanted to carry on teaching instead. I had found my "calling".

I believe it is important to try as many things as possible throughout your life. You never know what may be waiting down the path less travelled. Providence may indeed guide you there, but just in case, it does you no harm to keep an open mind.

Do you remember the board game Battleship? What a game. My brother and I had many a fight over it. I remember flinging the board and its pegs at him. It was only on the 88 that I realised how important Battleship might be.

Battleship, like life, is a game of trial and error to discover what floats your boat! It begins with an entirely blank board of X coordinates running vertically up the left side and blank Y coordinates running horizontally along the bottom. Your opponent locates battleships somewhere in this matrix of boxes – out of your sight, as you place yours also out of the opponent's view – and now with smug looks, you both peer over the board, each daring the other to find them.

At this early stage of the game it is impossible to know where your opponent's battleships are hidden. So initially it is all guesswork. Red and white pegs mark correct and incorrect guesses. The process of trial and error has begun. In this game the misses are as revealing as the hits. With every effort and every trial, you move closer to the goal; the location of a battleship.

Isn't life the same? With every effort and every trial, you draw closer to your calling, your passions, and your reasons for being. Some find out early in life, others much later. All efforts are appropriate and viable ways of playing the game.

As well as being given the chance to jaunt through life's rich fabric of opportunity, I concluded there was another reason that life never quite goes according to plan, namely that, if it did, how utterly predictable and dull life would be. In 1993 Bill Murray starred in the fantasy-comedy *Groundhog Day*. The film was about a TV weatherman who, while covering an annual Groundhog Day festival, finds himself trapped in a time loop destined to live the same day again and again and again. Although a comedy, it is actually quite disturbing and highlights, I think, why life never allows itself to be predicted precisely. If it were possible to choose the time, place, colour, shape, and exact outcome of any goal set, very soon, achievement would lose its lustre.

The Rio 2016 Olympics have just concluded as I write this. The efforts, world records, near misses and personal stories of toil and dedication have been inspiring, to say the least. Yet if every win were certain, would we be moved to emotion by the reports of athletic striving? It is life's unpredictability that makes it worth living; uncertainty the X factor that keeps us all coming back for more. The journey is indeed more important than the destination.

Yet old habits die hard, and while I was learning to relish the experiences of the journey, I had a destination to reach, a point to prove, and hypotheses to confirm or refute. As life-affirming as these detours had been, they were taking me further from my personal gold medal: finishing the 88 within a time and money limit. I hoped that I hadn't been given one diversion too many.

CHAPTER 11

The Power of Love

Does God (Universe or other) simply get tired of being alone,
And creates other than itself to be loved and to love?
Maybe that is what we are all about.
To be loved and to love.
To love in all its beautiful and far-reaching forms.
To love the sun bouncing off of the river's flow,
To the gentle breath of a lover kissing your neck.
From the unconditional kindness of a stranger to a lost traveller,
To the openness and love to accept the gift of a compliment.
Maybe that is what we are all about.
—*Journal entry*

"DON'T BE TOO busy walking to stop and share your heart."
Hajime had admonished. Though I had left Hajime-san many miles before, his words stayed with me every step of the way. He knew that I had goals to reach and points to prove, but he reminded me, time and again, not to miss the real heart of the 88: love and kindness. When he first told me, I heard his words, but it wasn't until much later that I understood them. In truth, it has taken almost ten years to integrate these ideas.

I am a fighter at heart, as are my mother and my grandfather before her. Aggression is entwined around the double helix of my DNA. Instinctively, my response to danger, trouble, negativity, or injustice is to fight, hackles up, against them. It is a curse, this primal response, albeit an effective one at times.

Unconditional love and impartial compassion are central to the practice of Buddhism, alongside meditation, and they are by far the most challenging states to achieve. My hardest battles have not been on the tatami mats of martial arts schools and *dojos* but in trying to penetrate a frozen and stoic heart.

Although I fall desperately short of the compassionate ideals shown by icons such as Mother Teresa and the Dalai Lama, I'm not quite the Tin Man from the Wizard of Oz either. I cried as a boy when I found my hamster, Vanilla, cardboard stiff in one of the pockets of the pool table, which had been dismantled and stored under the bunk beds after the Christmas holidays. Yet I didn't cry when Nanny Marce died. I had nightmares after visiting Nanny Mary in hospital and listened to her whirr through her throat after a tracheotomy, and I punched seven holes in the wardrobe door when Grandad Alb passed away. Still, to this day, years after his funeral, I feel pangs of guilt at not visiting Grandad John enough in the last years of his old and tired life. I regularly cry too at soppy films and at the parts where Gordon Ramsey reveals the restaurant-saving changes to tearful and grateful owners. Weighing this all up, I'll let you decide how open, or not, my heart is.

We are all at different stages of emotional maturity; some of us more "open" than others. Some of us laugh off fears about utility bills and mounting debts, whilst others wake up at 2.30 a.m. for months on end until a doctor's intervention is necessary for the stomach ulcer that has formed. Some deal with relationship problems by ignoring that they exist; others meet them head on, despite the tears and the shouting on the way to a resolution. Some leave early for work, inspired by the challenges ahead; others shrink into the seat of the bus, loathing every mile on the way to their job.

The routine of day-to-day living can be stifling. Whether it is the daily school run, the commute to work, another thousand words churned out as a writer, more reps as an athlete, more antibiotics to prescribe to yet another villager with sniffles at a countryside GP practice – the monotony of schedules is imprisoning. It's not that most of us don't love what we do; the passion that burnt when starting out at least still flickers somewhere in us. But society, as it is currently structured, pushes us to fit more into ever-shrinking segments of time, and few can avoid becoming jaded. Have you ever considered the absurdity of working countless hours to earn the money to take a break, a holiday from it all, once or twice a year?

This way of living shuts our hearts down too. Not the ones that cardiothoracic surgeons cut open to operate (although emotional frigidity is not good for health either) but that symbolic centre of our being that loves by all names: *agape*, *phileo*, *storge*, and *eros*, according to the ancient Greeks.

Get on any metro train in any major metropolis – London, Tokyo, Paris, New York – and note how everyone behaves. Eye contact is minimal; smiles are rare; friendly chit-chat not likely, not if you don't want to get arrested at the next stop as people call ahead to report a "crazy-talking murdering fool on the underground". So the grind turns our emotional hearts a little greyer with every year, and we save the vibrant red part for the ones we love at home. Except, often, the strain of our days cut off from humanity bubbles up and becomes a lethal concoction of frustration and rage that spills over and ends up hurting those closest to us – those who happen to be in the firing line of release as they stand open-armed, welcoming us home. Sadly it is a reality that many will recognise. We often hurt the ones we love.

One of the questions that hummed around my mind throughout the entire pilgrimage was: Is our basic nature essentially good, bad, or indifferent? Contrary to the belief that underlies and shapes so many of our modern systems – namely, that we are basically bad, flawed, and fallen from grace – Buddhist teachings stand tall in direct opposition. Buddhists believe that humans are basically good and are inherently wise. They call this state of being "Buddha nature". It is important to understand that the "good" in Buddha nature isn't in contrast to "bad". Buddhists teach there is no bad when it comes to human nature. The good of Buddha nature could be described instead as whole, pure, or complete.

One of the aims of the mindfulness meditation that I spoke about previously is to come to recognise this Buddha nature by observing it directly, proving the theory, so to speak. There are other, more extreme ways of being introduced to this state. The *keisaku* is a flat wooden paddle used for hitting monks, not as punishment for serious Buddhist transgressions (drinking fizzy drinks or killing mosquitos) but for a greater problem: drifting focus. Monks, while staring at blank walls meditating, are slapped on the shoulder with the paddle if the chief monk on duty notices an adept's mind wandering. Sagging posture and fidgeting are the giveaways, apparently. The sting is enough to haul the meditator's attention back from its fantasy land and onto the job at hand.

The *keisaku* whack is reported to be hard enough to warrant a sign over the head of some less hardy meditators: "'Do not hit," it reads. It is usually only found above the heads of those Western students in search of an "authentic" Japanese Zen experience. Those same students, with their preflight "selfies" and social posts, are quickly awakened to a truth, if not the one they were expecting: that spiritual practice is not as romantic as it at first seems. "Off to find myself in a Zen monastery in Japan. Life is good. Peace," their Facebook status may have read. Later it may have been updated to "Home now, with sore shoulders. I should have stayed at home. I didn't realise this spiritual work was such hard work!"

Some, mostly outsiders, criticise the use of the *keisaku*. They suggest it is psychopathic torture by monks demonstrating a lethal concoction of repressed emotion with too few outlets in which to express it. No doubt some fit this description – life is not perfect, after all – but this type of shock therapy has thwacked many students of Zen towards or completely into enlightened states.

In a *Zendō*, a *Zen* training hall, shock and surprise have been harnessed as teaching aids to direct students towards higher states for generations. Many of us non-students have also benefited from this tool too, albeit unknowingly. When the survivor of a sudden car crash suddenly realises how much he loves his wife and children and falls in love all over again, this is a type of enlightenment. When a new father stands in the hospital doorway looking on, awestruck, at the birth of his new baby, this is a type of enlightenment. When athletes play the game of their life, where time slows as do their opponent's countermoves, and every shot they take works seamlessly, this too is another form of enlightenment. With discursive thought momentarily suspended by circumstance, we are able to briefly glimpse this remarkable state – Buddha nature. With practice we observe that it is always present and available, even if during our busy days we fail to notice. It's there, humming in the background.

Walking the 88 is another way to encourage this innate and good state. With few distractions to obscure it, we allow our Buddha nature to take centre stage and let it start to open our hearts and encourage kindness. The first time on the pilgrimage that I felt a major positive shift in my heart was, ironically, right after I felt that it was broken beyond repair. I had just finished my prayers and rituals at Enkōji, Temple 39, and sat down to eat lunch. It wasn't the first time that I had felt alone while on pilgrimage, but this was different. It wasn't the faint homesickness I had experienced as an eighteen-year-old, away from home, teaching on summer camps in New York. Nor was it was like the other low points the pilgrimage had brought out in me. It was a profound and penetrating sadness, edging on trip-cancelling depression. I was tired of striving for the end; fatigued at the discipline necessary to keep placing one foot in front of another in search of answers that I could not guarantee. It was hard for me to remember a time in my life when I had felt this depressed, and it felt as if had come out of the blue.

As a teacher, most of my work is done centre stage. However, by nature I'm an introvert and a very private person. I like people, but I'm happy with my own thoughts and space; I'm not a fan of group banter. Time alone, ordinarily, doesn't unsettle me, yet then and there, I just wanted – actually needed – the company of another human being.

And she appeared. Takako. The most peculiar-looking girl you have ever seen in your life. Kitted out in all the shop bought regalia of a pilgrim, she looked like a comical caricature of Buddhism. It's strange how some people exude natural style, and some people don't. You could put David Beckham in a cloth sack, and he would still look killer handsome, and you could measure up Takako with all the correct gear, and it would always look a little wonky, ill-fitting, and scruffy. Blind as a bat, she squinted from under her conical pilgrim hat that kept slipping down over her face. Uninvited, she plunked down next to me and with a mouth full of more teeth than I think there should have been, she smiled the warmest, most beautiful smile. I loved her immediately.

Most people's initial reactions to declarations of love, if honest, are assumptions that they are discussing eros: that love type characterised by intense passion, romance, and sex. The giddy love felt at the beginning of many new relationships. In our modern world, it is this superficial love that takes precedence, and it is a little sad. I think Takako would laugh as loud as I if she thought that it was this that people thought we had going on between us.

Takako talked a lot. It wasn't the selfish talk of a person trying to proselytize, filling up space with their thoughts, opinions and views, but that of someone excited and fascinated by life. I felt as if I had known her for a lifetime, and her friendliness was an instant remedy for the dark and unexpected sadness and loneliness that had descended on me.

"I'm studying engineering at University in Osaka", she told me between attempts at straightening her wonky hat. "I have always wanted to walk the *hachi jū hachi,* to try and be a better person, so I thought I'd try. I'll do half now, in this term break, and then the other half another time."

Many Japanese do this, splitting up the walk into more manageable parts. Some of them are unable to create the time in their schedules, or the belief in themselves, to attempt the whole thing at once. When I admitted that I would be trying to do all 1,400 kilometres in one push, Takako said it was wonderful, *"Sugoi"*, and celebrated my ambition. There was not a trace of envy or competition, just pure and genuine support of my plight.

We walked for several hours and visited temples together. We shared stories of our past and hopes for the future and compared ideas about life, religion, and meaning. It is one of the most beautiful things about pilgrimage; meeting people along the way who share a common goal, people with whom we don't share any other emotional baggage. It is these sporadic communions that reaffirm a faith and belief in community and kindness so often lost in the impersonal jungles of a modern metropolis.

When I first started, I wasn't so open to these impromptu meets. I walked head down, wanting to be left alone to complete the number of walking miles I had set myself for each day. Yet as the days wore on, I welcomed and looked forward to the company and camaraderie, for the opportunity to share and the chance to learn. I didn't need it particularly – aside from the day Takako came to my emotional rescue – so the anticipation of communion was never needy, but it was always appreciated and welcomed. It was good, for a change, not to be living in a vacuum of solitude, one I think I had grown a bit too used to surviving in since my days as a competitive athlete. Takako taught me that a kind smile is a beautiful thing and possibly life-saving – an important lesson for a world obsessed by looks, appearance, and the superficialities of celebrity. This lesson has greater significance for me now after watching my own daughter battle an eating disorder driven by the need to "look better" and to "fit in". I learnt about kindness from Takako's example. It is something I still aspire to today. Yet, gratefully, I would have the chance to teach her something too.

Takako loved paraphernalia. If she were a camper, she would be one of those who have every piece of camping gadgetry. Spork (spoon and fork), flint stick (just use matches, why don't you?), portable clothesline (er, string?), and the latest non-rip, non-drip tent that will undoubtedly rip and drip at the first sign of a storm. She also loved her guidebook and map. Every few hundred yards, it seemed, we would stop so that Takako could consult her guidebook and map, in the same way that many of us constantly check our smart phones.

"Takako-san, why do you keep checking your map?" I asked her.

"To see where we are going, Mattō-san," she beamed back.

It was time to pay forward some of the pilgrimage wisdom that Hajime had gifted to me miles before.

"Put the map away, Takako. Let's just walk and ask the heavens to guide us. Trust them. We'll get where we need to go." For the first time I saw her smile break, and even, I think, noticed a slight panic on her face.

"Mattō-san, this is very difficult. It is very easy to get lost here.

Shikoku is a huge island, and we may not find the next temple. I think we should use the map."

Shikoku is indeed a tricky place to navigate. Though the route of the 88 is basically a circuit around an island, the temples don't fit perfectly around the periphery. They cut back inland here, sit on the edges of capes there. Occasionally small estuaries need to be traversed, and double-backs into forest or bamboo copses are not unusual. The Japanese authorities' love affair with concrete and "Governmental development projects" is mostly to blame. They will concrete anything in the name of "progress". What was once a way forward is now a concrete wall. The 88 temple pilgrimage route is always being forced to change.

I love Japan, but I mourn the decimation of its remarkable and diverse wildlife. Countless species of flora and fauna have been taken to the edge of extinction and beyond. Budgets, red tape, and less than coordinated planning are destroying much of its natural beauty. Japan is trapped by consumerism and the never-ending production of stuff, as is the rest of the world. When I first visited, years ago, I didn't want to admit that it was true of a land I had held so highly in my mystical imaginings, but it was, and is, and it took me a long time to accept this brutal and disappointing truth.

Complexities of modern-day development aside, the other problem with navigating the 88 temple pilgrimage was the signposting. The 88 main temples and more than 100 smaller worship sites – *bangai* – dotted around a 1,400-kilometre circumference, are signposted mostly by little stickers. An icon of a red stick man pilgrim is attached randomly, it appeared, on lamp posts, walls, trees, and stakes jabbed into the ground. Very occasionally a town council has budgeted for a stone-crafted milestone, like those on Roman roads of old. Finding these was always an exciting moment and nearly always celebrated with a photograph.

Intentionally or not, the 88's methods of signposting around the island is almost completely unreliable, and it leaves the pilgrim with an important choice, one that I would point out to Takako. Do you continue to stress and strain in search of the sticky land-markers, cross referencing them with your map and triple checking against the guidebook information, or just relax, enjoy the scenery, and trust that the heavens will guide and direct when necessary?

She baulked at the idea of faith, at first, as many would. It's hard to give up the habit of control that dominates so many lives. "Trust me", I asked her, and she did, and I in turn trusted the heavens to guide us both. "Don't let me down", I pleaded skyward, "now that I've sung your praises to my new friend."

For the rest of the journey we walked, talked, laughed, and enjoyed shared humanity, and we practised trust, because isn't trust another type of kindness? We trusted to look up at just the right time, height, and direction to notice one of the pilgrim stickers pointing the way forward. We believed that we'd bump into a local who would know exactly where to find the next temple. We trusted to see a crumpled flyer at our feet, with just the information we needed to locate the next *bangai*. As with all things, trust, faith, and the art of letting go (and it is an art) become easier with practice. We weren't lost the whole day. That always helps build confidence in a process.

Finally, as with all relationships forged while on pilgrimage, it was time to go our separate ways, to continue our personal journeys, and to fulfil our unique rhythms, destinies, and needs. We would walk on, alone but not lonely, enriched by time with a friend. I'd almost forgotten how important friendships could be.

Takako gave me a *tenugui* – a Japanese head scarf used for anything and everything from protecting heads from the sun, drying hands, mopping brows, and wrapping presents - and I gave her a huge hug and deep, respectful bow. The doorway of my heart was a little more open for having met her and I wondered if the heavens had sent her – the angel of the 88 – with her invisible wings and wonky pilgrim's hat.

Takako had opened the door, but others would step through it to help me refine my understanding of the teachings on kindness and compassion. In Kagawa Ken now, the forest trail opened up into a clearing with beds of roses and a small greenhouse. Daiki-san looked up from tending his roses and waved to me. We went into the greenhouse where Aiko-san, his wife, served us tea and *umeboshi* (Japanese salt plums). Daiki-san was an *Oshō*, a Buddhist priest in training. Over lunch he taught me that the kindness, evolved while on the 88, is said to counteract in part the negativity of the world at large. Kōbō Daishi himself is said to have taught that 100,000 recitations of the Hannya Shingyō – the Heart Sutra prayer prayed temple side - would bring enlightenment and world peace. I left Daiki and Aiko contemplating the work still left to do, on so many different levels.

As the days wore on, the walking miles and Hannya Shingyō recitations piled up. Honestly, I don't know why I was feeling calmer, kinder, and more open and free, but I was. Undoubtedly the continued kindness of others played a big part: like the time it poured rain all day, and a lady in a café gave me her umbrella to take with me; like the assistants in a jewellery shop who spent almost an hour and a half rushing between computers and laptops to print off bits and pieces of maps to ease my journey; like the old lady who insisted that I sit with her a while ("Pilgrims can't walk all day, you know") and drink green tea while she picked me three bright orange, delicious *natsumikan* from the tree in her front garden. I have never tasted oranges as flavourful as these. Is it possible that they were infused with the taste of her kindness?

The willingness of people to help another, in harsh and tough times, is music to the soul. It confirms that life and living are good, as Buddhists purport. It is an ideal worth striving for, especially in these times troubled by terror and violence. Of course, I'm not naïve enough to think that smiles and prayers are enough to secure peace, but they are a beginning – the smiles at least. The global community is but a collection of peoples all wanting to be happy. If we concentrate on what we can affect – our own kindness to ourselves and others – then this multiplied can bring major change: "one step", to use Hajime's advice.

From the experiences that I enjoyed while on the 88, I conclude that life is on our side. It loves us. I believe it does. Maybe sometimes, we just need to let it in. This is easier said than done, I understand. When driven by schedules, causes, and goals, it is easy to walk by and miss those that have shown up in our lives: "I haven't the time"; "Sorry, can't stop, we'll catch up later"; "Not now, mate, I'm busy." My first instinct, certainly, was to favour completing my task over the meeting and greeting of others. The devil on my shoulder reminded me that love and communion are all very well, but if this trip didn't get completed, on time and on budget, then I would have failed. I would prove, in my failure, that life and its outcomes are not of my making; free will, merely a myth. "Forget love, Matt", continued the devil; "hurry on and cross the finish line; show us all that we can reach our goals and achieve our dreams."

But what of love and friendship in all this pushing, reaching, and striving? Can we not have both? Now there is a worthy goal.

CHAPTER 12

You Knew It All Along

Within silence, truth is revealed.
—*Journal entry*

S TEP AWAY FROM the book; there is nothing to learn here.

They say that writers experience everything twice, once when they live the live version, and again when they write about it. It's true; at least it has been for me. Pilgrimage is hard, long, difficult, emotionally challenging, but also satisfying and rewarding. So too is writing a book, running a marathon, completing a business plan, raising a family, fighting for a marriage to work, finishing a dissertation, flying to the moon, or climbing the stairs with the weight of years; everything and anything is a pilgrimage of sorts.

We can choose for the journey to be hard and stressful. We endure these types of trips rather than embrace them. On this path, we constantly look to others for approval and guidance, failing to trust our inherent abilities to smooth the way. We doubt our strength to strive courageously into the unknown. Time and again we deny our intelligence to fathom near-impossible complexity and forget our talent to pioneer seemingly impossible challenges. We rely on others' experience to enrich our own, trusting their authority and judgement better than our own. We buy into the erroneous belief of limited faculties, limited talent, limited worth, limited skills, limited abundance, and limited time. If only we had more of it all, life would be grand. Sound familiar? The circle of this pilgrimage is closing.

We give up both faith and responsibility for ourselves when we sign up to the next course of classes to a guru dishing out great advice. We are left broken and stranded when we find that our Messiah's advice doesn't quite bring us to the holy land we had thought it would. We are even more devastated by the discovery that our leader is merely human, one who has simply evolved a set of skills in one area of life but may well have fallen from grace in others. When we forget that we are born of the same source, from the same talent pool as our guides, we replace individual creativity with mimicry. Our faculties of personal evolution then become atrophied by lack of use. We live our lives in the shadows of others – a grim, dark, and cold choice indeed. This is the danger of living your life through others' experience rather than your own.

I remember upsetting one of two assessors regarding this issue, during the final examinations of my professional tennis coach's course. Philip was a short, rotund man whose massive ego made him highly objectionable and unapproachable. Philip loved being an assessor, not out of a passion for sharing knowledge but for the platform it allowed him to wield power over others. He reminded me of some officers in American TV reality police programmes. Many of these officers were committed and honourable members of a force doing a difficult job, while others clearly relished the power and control that come with a badge of authority. My other assessor and tutor, Keith, was the polar opposite, and he was and still is an inspiration to me. Keith changed the way I viewed coaching and taught me, by example, that those who know little talk loudest, protesting their truths vehemently, while those who know most often stand aside quietly, smiling, eyes gleaming, gently fiddling with the strings of their tennis racket, letting others preach.

One of the final exam questions asked: "What is the future for teaching and coaching?" My answer: "That it is as good as redundant." I know it sounds like a failing response for a coaching and teaching degree question, but I had given this much thought, then and since. We have nothing to teach and nothing to learn. I believe, as I told Keith and Philip, that ultimately each of us must find our own truths and patent our own discoveries; it would be impossible to do otherwise. We are all so unique that our view of the world, given all of our personal perspectives, experiences, and viewpoints, can never be fully understood by another. Any guidance, therefore, can only be an opinion of our unique view.

Who can prescribe definitive measures to lives with so many individual variables? Lives that others know so little about. In some ways this is a frightening realisation. At least it was for me initially. But later I started to see that this was the very gift of life, uncertain, creative, open-ended, and without limit, ours to discover and ours alone. But what of teaching, is it redundant? Well, not entirely, but it was fun to watch Philip squirm at my answer and Keith chuckle quietly away in the corner, silently proud of his protégé.

Almost twenty-five years on in a teaching career, I believe it is our job, as educators, teachers, leaders, friends, and family, to bring those in search of learning to an environment in which they can safely discover, learn, fail, and succeed their way to new heights of understanding that will enrich their lives. Teach a man to fish rather than feed him one, so to speak. It is only through self-discovery and the rich process of trial, error, and improvement that we develop both confidence in our worth and the faith to create the life of our choosing. With burgeoning confidence comes an understanding not only that manifesting in life's playground is fun, but also that we are duty bound to do it. What's more, we must also help others enjoy the same process. It is more fun to share our successes than hoard them.

Creating our outcomes doesn't have to be an arduous, tortuous haul, unless, of course, we choose for it to be. Do you want to believe that? Are you prepared to give up your idea that life is a hard, long, and perilous slog? Would you like to believe that it could be smooth, effortless, and instantaneous? Discovering our inner strength, the power that has been with us all along, is like walking into a dark room and turning on the light. The contents were there all along; you were just unable to see them. With the light on you instantly see that the room is full of opportunities, and this is not a gradual process. Before you were blind, but now you see, and all manner of choices are yours to make. Sit on the sofa, or don't; watch the TV, or not; strum the guitar in the corner of the room, or use the strings to floss your teeth – who cares? Only you. And it's all OK.

Approaching the end of my pilgrimage I wrote this entry in my journal:

> There is nowhere to get to because you are already there; you have already arrived. So, just place your attention on the moment and enjoy.

But I hadn't yet arrived. Here in the "real world", I was still just a man virtually broke, with many miles left to walk and just six days in which to walk them. Failure to complete my task would disprove that I was unlimited and instead prove that time and money were, ultimately, the masters that steered the direction of the boats of our dreams. And it would as good as kick God into touch.

Yet it was here on Shikoku's pilgrimage that I had begun to trust the heavens whose hand I was calling on them to show, and they had. To date, for me at least, their help, love, and guidance were irrefutable, but old habits die hard. With the end in sight, parts of the "old me" – that red-blooded, goal-driven human who had spent longer living away from the 88 than walking on it – continued to doubt, stress, and strain. I am a work in progress, as we all are, and although familiar behaviour reared its head, this time rather than encourage it, I just let it be. Instead I continued to try to believe that the heavens had my best interests at heart and, if they were a worthy power, would help me cross the finishing line.

So I pulled up my bootstraps and kept walking. The profound experiences kept coming thick and fast. One day, the rhythm of my steps rocked me into a near hypnotic state where I experienced time's ability to alter and bend. In the foothills of the thickly forested Mount Ishizuchi, at Temple 64 – Maegamiji – day turned to night and I suddenly realised that I had been walking for fourteen hours without pause. I would have bet money that I had only been walking thirty minutes or so, maximum. It was a strange sensation. Mount Ishizuchi is the highest peak in Western Japan, and it is told that Kōbō Daishi himself had spent time at its summit performing ritual, fasting, prayer, and meditation. I wondered if a little of its power was working on me. My perception of time changed drastically from then on.

I had countless moments of déjà vu, recollections of past dreams, and a certain feeling that I knew this new place, although I'd never visited it before. All of these moments made me start to examine more the Buddhist belief in reincarnation. I am still uncertain about this concept, but I know what I experienced on the 88, and who am I to discount as crazy and deluded, greater minds than mine – those of Buddhist leaders? A keystone strength of Buddhism is its insistence on experience and practice to confirm understanding of its principles. Tibetan Buddhist monks practise regular debating of the teachings so that they don't fall into the trap of blind belief. Buddhism is a system that has thought long and hard about its messages to the world and continues to do so.

I continued to meet beautiful people. I had cake and sweets with a Buddhist priest, his wife, and their son, who taught me that celibacy is not a requirement of all schools of Buddhism. As I sat with them in the basement of their home, I watched them operate like every other "regular" family – teasing, discussing, showing affection, organising, sharing – the only difference being that, in the morning, Dad would kiss his family and leave for work, not in an office but in a temple. His work: to teach others the dharma, the way of the Buddha. He invited me to the evening sermon, and I gratefully accepted, although I did not understand much of the complex Japanese terminology and language used. No problem; its essence was clear, no matter the language. This family left me with the hope that those who love their partners and families can still benefit from the highest levels of spiritual teaching, asceticism not being a prerequisite to lasting happiness.

Outside Temple 80, Kokubunji, where in 741 Emperor Shōmu decreed that a monastery and nunnery should be built, believing that the Buddhist faith would ensure both the happiness and peace of Japan, I met a monk performing *takahatsu*. *Takahatsu* is a traditional practice whereby ascetics stand outside temple grounds, often for many hours, reciting sutra in return for food from beneficiaries of the prayer. It made me consider the rigours of a pure religious life. I wondered if I could or should do it. I would settle for walking the pilgrimage, for now at least.

And soon, I would meet Rei and Tomoki.

Rays of early morning sun striped into the room of the *ryōkan* I had saved up to stay in before starting out on the last leg of the 88. Several days of living under playground slides, on park benches, or in temple grounds and eating food gifted to me by locals, allowed me to save enough of the money I had left to enjoy one last stay in a traditional Japanese inn.

I love *ryōkan*s. They are an echo and enshrinement of a Japan long gone; a romantic Japan, a Japan I had been in love with since that fateful exhibition back in London all those years ago. Simplicity and space define them. Rooms are large and light with only essential furniture: floor height table and chairs during the day, futons and bedding at night. Sliding doors hide floor to ceiling wall cupboards that hide excess, out of view until needed. Beautiful intricate murals, the only notable decorations of the room, often adorn doors. Trinkets, bits and pieces and keepsakes have no place in a *ryōkan* room, for they are seen to clutter the space, the mind, and the emotions.

The *Tokonama*, a dedicated area, is the only "excess" in the chamber. Usually referred to as the *Toko*, this alcove is an essential and defining part of traditional Japanese interior design. On display within this small but unmissable space, is any number of items: stunning calligraphy scrolls, both religious and not, Ikebana Zen flower arrangements, meticulous bonsai features, and *Okimono* – religious ornaments. I love *Tokonama*s. More than that, I love what people choose to display in them. They never fail to lift the heart and enliven the spirit.

Choosing to enjoy the *ryōkan* brought up some interesting questions. Many of the insights and maturations that seem to happen while on pilgrimage do so via the hardship, frugality, and simple living that the walk demands. Watching the monk perform *takahatsu* confirmed that hardship is considered a means to happiness in many walks of life. But does it have to be this way? Are the complexities and splendours of modern living not just another, albeit different, expression of life? One of many plucked from the source of infinite variation? Must we renounce them to be at peace? Is accumulation such a bad thing? Does suffering equal holiness? If so, why? It all seemed a bit harsh to me. So I decided to treat myself to this last night of luxury before pressing on to the final temples. The meal served felt like I imagined the experience of the Last Supper to be: a final opportunity for luxury, pampering, and self-cherishing before taking on the final battle, the last green mile toward a truth that I may or may not be equipped to handle.

I awoke the next morning after a dreamless sleep. Time was running out: I had a flight in Osaka waiting for me, now in just three days' time, and the last of my coins rattled around in my pocket. I was on my last legs during this last leg. I pulled on my walking boots over swollen feet and ankles and slowly walked – because I was unable to do it at any other speed – out onto the road. These first few steps of every morning were excruciating as the bones in my feet, ankles, knees, and hips creaked and twisted back into an alignment that would allow another day of hard locomotion. It had been this way since the second day. The sun was rising, and mist hung around the base of surrounding mountains. The air was fresh with the cold of a February morning in Japan. All was well with the world today. The finish line was beckoning.

There are 88 temples on the 88 temple pilgrimage; who knew, right? But actually, the old school route has 98, from number 1 to 88, then back through 10, 9, 8, etc., and culminating in the closing of the circuitous pilgrimage by ending up where you started at Temple 1. Around thirty-eight kilometres are added to the trip if you do it this way. I didn't know this little fact until the day before my final push. To be true to my nature, I would have to make this addition to my journey if it was to be an authentic one, and if nothing else, I wanted it to be authentic. This nugget of information threw a proverbial spanner into the works, and any last thoughts that I might humanly be able to manipulate a winning end to this trip were dashed. I was now totally in the hands of the gods. Faith was the only tool left in my box. For now, I had put this out of my mind; fretting would only besmirch this wonderful morning. I was determined to enjoy the summit of the trip, to relish the last temples leading up to Ōkuboji, Temple 88 – the "temple of the fulfilment of wishes". As I walked between Shidōji,

Temple 85, with its bright red pagoda, and Nagaoji, Temple 86, with its dusty courtyard and perfectly manicured avenue of trees, I noticed a shadow catching up with mine.

"Ohaiyō gozaimasu." A girl, I guessed in her mid-twenties, greeted me good morning. Her name was Juna. Juna wore none of the religious paraphernalia I had seen other Japanese wearing. Instead, she opted for camouflage combat fatigues, T-shirt, a sweater that stayed tied to her waist, and a red paisley bandana that kept her long, silky black hair off of her face. I wondered if she was hiding or denying her incredible beauty. There was a story here, beneath what my eyes could see, but my limited Japanese couldn't uncover it. As we spent time walking together, her hard shell softened until all that remained of it was the masculine attire. Lives change while walking a pilgrimage, if only in subtle ways. As with Takako earlier, I felt immediately at home and comfortable with Juna, but where a sexual interest in Takako was an equally ludicrous thought for us both, physical attraction to Juna was not out of the question.

Which brings us neatly to sex and its place in our world, religion, and public opinion. When I say neatly, can it ever really be? Few subjects cause as much trouble for people to discuss. Few subjects are as messy (every pun intended). I thought back again to my coffee and sweets with the Zen monk and his wife and son. Why can some religions accept sex while others cannot? Ultimately, all religions, I believe, are in search of higher meaning and insights into life's mysteries, so how is it that they arrive at such contrasting conclusions while traversing the same terrain? How can something as fundamental to life's continuation as procreation be besmirched as sinful? Why is sex so freely used as a weapon both in and out of relationships? Why is something so natural and enjoyable considered so wrong?

Like all things, it depends on the angle from which you approach the subject. The endless hours of thinking, contemplating, and musing while on the 88 kept me coming back to the thought that, inherently, things are neither good nor bad. They just are. We are the ones who attach meaning to them based on the spectacles we are viewing the world through: spectacles shaped by experience, habits, and beliefs handed down from generation to generation.

Things mean different things to different people; sex is such an obvious example. To some, gay sex is a sin and an aberration; to others it is a beautiful expression of commitment between a couple very much in love. Some see sex as a way to pay the bills and put food on the table, others as a way to unwind at the end of a hard day's work – work that also pays the bills and puts food on the table. For some a gentle touch creates a flinch and memories of a past where gentleness erupted into violence while for others, a similar touch creates feelings of support, respect, and care. For yet others, the ache for touch needs to be upgraded to the lash of a whip, maybe?

If I learnt nothing else while on pilgrimage, I learnt that life is never clear-cut. It is a rich tapestry of views, opinions, perceptions, and ideas. We all believe we are right until learning that we aren't. And ultimately, we all want to be happy, just going about it in different ways. Life is not easy. But it is simple. We are born; we die. Somewhere in between, we express life. Somewhere in between, we also try to figure out death because we are most likely afraid of it. The mayfly, we assume, is unaware that its life after emerging from the cocoon is just a short one, but the double-edged gift of conscious thought means that we have years of life to worry about the death that comes at the end of it all. Inevitable and frightening, it is made worse by clinging to the very thing that cannot be secured eternally: human life. To the Buddhists, the thing that underlies both life and death, the thing that survives them all, is Buddha nature, and its first quality, they say, is universal, impartial, compassionate love. It is a love that is not desirous or needy, expectant or demanding, aggressive or wanting, limited or provisional. It is, actually, quite lovely.

This idea was something I had been aware of for many years. I just didn't fully understand it. Yes, of course, it is not a difficult idea to comprehend intellectually; I was just unable to actualise it in practice (I understand how guitar chords work too, but, trust me, I'm no Jimi Hendrix), but this started to change on the 88. I don't know how or why; after all, pilgrimage is only a very long walk scattered with temple visits and prayer. Yet I started to experience a warm friendliness toward almost everyone I met, even the few grumpy old codgers whom I would have previously wished harm. I was starting to have a sense of the universal, impartial, compassionate love the Buddhists exalt. And it was confirmed when I met Juna.

When we finally reached the gates of Ōkuboji, Temple 88, we both bowed; the end was near. Ōkuboji was the final temple before returning to the first, and it was a momentous arrival.

The temple is built at the foot of two mountains (one of them, Mount Nantai, is 776 metres high) that represent two important symbols of esoteric Buddhism. Walking along the paved way leading to the main temple hall, Juna reached for my hand. We held hands all around the temple grounds, laughing like excited schoolchildren with the joy of having nearly completed a mammoth task. We stopped at an ornate turquoise column atop a glass room filled with *Kōngō zue,* the walking staff of the pilgrim said to be the embodiment of Kōbō Daishi himself. Although I hadn't walked with one (I couldn't afford one), Juna had, and, as customary, she placed hers into the room with the hundreds of others as thanks for having completed her journey safely.

We continued to hold hands as we recited our prayers at the main hall, and if people were watching us on CCTV, they might have assumed that we were very much in love. In a way, we were, but not as you think. The love we shared that day had not one iota of the limits of a physical, desirous romantic relationship. It was a bigger, richer, deeper love; it was universal, impartial, and compassionate. And it would have been shared with anyone who shared that moment with us, whether young, old, rich, poor, man, or woman. Looking out from the temple grounds at the mist-covered mountains, we felt that ominous time for separation arise. Like all things, this beautiful moment must pass too. Juna and I hugged as we said our goodbyes. Her journey would end here. Mine was to take me back to Ryōzenji, Temple 1. My life and, I hope, hers were richer for this experience.

The walk from Temple 88 to Temple 1 is a long one that leaves much time to reflect on the past thirty days; thirty days of walking the equivalent of a marathon and a half every day; a journey that pushes the body, the mind, the emotions, and, for those who believe in such a thing, the spirit. I had learnt so much while being here on this great trip, but lessons were still to come.

One question that kept coming back to me time and again was regarding "free will". I am aware of the concept that we are free to pick any and all life of our choosing and that we all do, either consciously or otherwise. But is there actually a preferred quality for us to aspire to? Does life care how we opt to live? Many people have chosen kindness and been successful; many have chosen malice with the same degree of competence; others have mastered the art of indifference. Would life prefer us to choose one over the other? I'm still asking this question today, years after the pilgrimage, but I have my suspicions, maybe just hopes, that we are inherently good. I hope so.

The Buddhists believe it. They say that our real essence is one of non-attached love and compassion. Is it a choice they have made, or a genuine insight into life's most profound quality, a quality that ultimately provides meaning, guidance, and direction for us all? I am many miles from knowing a definitive answer for myself. I may never know the answer, but two people I met in the last days of the 88 moved me forward in my search. I met Rei and Tomoki on the road between Temple 88 and Temple 10. We exchanged the usual pleasantries that pilgrims share when their paths cross: How are you feeling? How long have you been walking today/this week/so far, in total? Why are you walking?

Tomoki was walking to ease the sense of burn-out that had worsened with every year of his last ten as a "salaryman", a corporate pawn to a Japanese company, bound by the order and regulation the company demands. He looked much older than he should have at forty-one and was thin and scrawny with stress. He had taken his full holiday allowance in one go, so that he could spend two months walking the 88 and try to bring back some heart and soul to his life.

Rei, a family friend of Tomoki, was walking for an altogether different reason. Her sister was dying of ovarian cancer. The doctors were unable to offer much hope, so Rei had turned to the temples to see if the gods could intervene. She offered her efforts of walking, prayer, and mantra recitation as a last-ditch attempt to help her cherished sibling, one she had played with as a child in the stream at the end of their garden. Rei said that she could still feel the water on her skin when she turned her mind back.

Rei and Tomoki touched my heart deeply. Both were shattered by life's show of cruelty, but rather than giving up, they had turned to the pilgrimage for help. I wanted to help too, if I could. Tomoki walked a slow and tired pace that was adding hours to the journey, but it didn't bother me; being with them was more important than sprinting for the line. I was grateful for the opportunity to be able to assist, in what little way that I could, joining Rei at each of the ten remaining temples and helping her by doubling up the prayers for her sister. Hey, you never know; it may work. There was very little to lose and much to gain.

I was prepared to concede that the restrictions of time and money were indeed very real, but the consolation would be greater; life-affirming life lessons I would take home with me. Yet technically, there was still time left to complete my task, and I had seen other miracles worked here on the 88, so all was not lost, just not under my control. With the realisation that it is impossible to know an outcome, peace often comes. Although I had been to the first ten temples at the beginning of my walk, I was now revisiting them with new eyes, arguably even an entirely new me. Here I was walking the same grounds, but as a different person, touched by the lessons, experiences, and realisations of the 88. Through this journey I had evolved in many ways, and I think I am a much better person for it.

There was little talk between us all as we walked and prayed our way through the last temples, just tears sometimes, but mostly hope for a healthy outcome for Rei's sister. The thought of death is sobering, but it is a subject that we must all face eventually. Buddhism encourages regular contemplation of death, and I struggled to face my own fears in this regard, initially. But far from being pessimistic, it actually brings solace and a degree of peace once you finally stop running from the thoughts about the inevitable. Introspection then leads to new understanding driven by calm consideration, rather than fears born of ignorance and denial. In these final miles it was clear that everything beginning must end, in every way.

We were finally back at Temple 1, Ryōzenji, exactly thirty days after I had started. My flight back to the UK would leave Osaka airport later that afternoon. God knows how I had done it, but I had; he had, more likely. Honestly, I had no idea how this was possible. Every calculation along the way had suggested that I would be hours, if not days off schedule by the time I had returned to Ryōzenji. But I had learnt on the 88 to expect the unexpected, no matter how bizarre, surreal, or unlikely. And I had learnt to trust powers far greater than mine.

It had been dark when I first set out to walk 1,400 kilometres, and I had seen nothing of this magnificent place. The *sōmon*, the gateway that stands as entrance to Japanese temple sites, was built of wood, flanked on either side by two wooden statues of Fudō Myōō, the wrathful protector deity. I love wood and anything built with it. I think, sometimes, that I can hear and feel it breathing. Wood brings life to a structure. The wooden *sōmon* gate at Ryōzenji was old; I don't know how old, but in its gnarled and weather-beaten cracks and folds lay the memories of years. I couldn't help but run my hands over the wood and smell its unmistakable smell.

We walked across the little bridge over the huge koi ponds to the main hall. It was stunning. Hundreds of lanterns hung from the ceiling, bathing the hall and everyone in its light. It was a physical display of enlightenment – a perfect symbol for the completion of the 88 temple pilgrimage. In that moment, I felt God.

Rei, Tomoki, and I prayed together one last time. Then, as always on the 88, we said goodbye to continue our personal journeys. There were tears in Rei's eyes when we hugged. No words were needed to explain both her gratitude to me and mine to her, for the opportunity to open my heart and practice compassion, possibly the greatest lesson of the 88. I hoped with all my heart that the prayers would make a difference. She handed me a white envelope, and I bowed my farewells to them both. As I waved them off, I stayed a little longer by myself at Ryōzenji, not quite ready to leave this place behind.

So there I was, back at Temple 1. I had closed the circle and now had indeed completed the 88 temple pilgrimage, walking it in the ways of old, on foot. I wrote this in my journal:

> With an empty physical victory to hand
> The truth dawns,
> That the goal is not the win,
> But the "nowness" of creating it.

It was not an anticlimax, as such, but more a deep understanding that the journey is more important than the destination, that the love and the lessons learnt along the way are more important than the discovery of ultimate truths, and that this journey would continue long after I had walked away from Ryōzenji, Japan, and returned to my "normal" life.

With the very last of my money that I had set aside purposefully for this moment, I walked to the main office to buy the *goshuin*. A *goshuin* is a single piece of paper on which the priest of the temple (for a 300-yen fee) stamps and then hand brushes the temple name in calligraphy. It serves as a record of temples visited, and ideally, a pilgrim collects one at each of the 88 temples. Considering my budget, I purchased just two: at Temple 1 and Temple 88. The calligraphy is a work of art, crafted in the poise of meditation. Leaving and walking back across the bridge over the koi pond, I stopped and looked deep into the water at the white, black, and orange koi that swam within. I became lost in the rhythm of their flow. I was neither thinking about the pilgrimage, now complete, nor planning my next step; I wasn't happy, or sad; I simply was.

I don't know how long I had been there staring into the pond's hypnotic ripples, but it was time to leave. There was still a four-hour trip (one train and two buses) to the airport, but there was a problem. A big problem. I had spent my last yen on the *goshuin* and had nothing left. I had known this situation was coming. As I knew that time was running out, I was more than aware that so too was money. But I had handed this challenge over to the heavens miles before. Except, it seemed, they hadn't delivered on this occasion.

You have got to be kidding me! After all this, would it be a money technicality that prevented the trip from being an utter success? Fourteen hundred kilometres in thirty days with £300, but now stranded without the bus and train fares to take me back to the airport at its conclusion.

Really? I felt the old familiar habit of rage start to bubble inside, but I stopped. And smiled, albeit ironically. It seemed that money, if not time, would be my downfall after all. Now, I felt the massive sinking of disappointment, when just twenty minutes earlier I had been immersed in the most profound state of peace and calm. How immediate the change from one emotion to another, as life gives with one hand and seemingly, takes with the other. This slip from high to low had been a common theme throughout the journey; so close, yet still so far.

I wondered at this as I leaned back against the bus shelter I had walked to, and stuffed my hands in my pocket. My thoughts were interrupted by something against my fingers. It was the envelope that Rei had given to me. I pulled it out and opened it up. Inside was a note: *"Mattō-san. Dōmo Arigatō Gozaimasu. Gambatte Kudasai."* Accompanying a note that simply said thank you and take care was a neat pile of yen notes. I cried as I unfurled them to find 2,000 yen – precisely the bus and train fares that I would need to make it back to the airport. The kindness of this *o-settai*, this monetary offering, was magic enough, but the miracle was that I had never told either Rei or Tomoki of my transport plans, my financial situation, or the flight I would need to catch to complete my journey. She had much more on her mind than my needs. I was staggered; this was utterly beyond belief. I looked skyward and smiled (after apologising for my doubt).

It is a long journey by bus and train back to Osaka airport from the island of Shikoku, home of the 88 temple pilgrimage, as it was a long journey around a pilgrimage that, in so many ways, was life affirming. I had managed to complete a dream despite having neither ample time nor money to do it. I had thrown a theory at the wall to see if it would stick: that time and money are a human-created obstacle, not a universal truth, and needn't limit the lives of our choosing. Of course, such claims will be open to both ridicule and contempt. I'm ready for the doubters. Experience will arm me against the onslaught of their criticism. "All of it just happy coincidence", I'm sure the Charlies of this world will tell me if they ever read this story. If they believe me, so be it. If they don't, no matter.

With my pilgrimage complete and forty minutes to spare before my flight, I thought I would try my credit card again at the duty-free, to buy some presents for my children. Just for kicks. I was ready to put it all back once the assistant told me my card was still being declined, but instead she smiled, handed me my receipt and the gifts, and wished me a safe journey. Now that I had survived walking the 88 frugally, as monks of old did, I no longer needed the safety net of my card, and it had been returned to me. It reminded me of a line from the film *Nanny McPhee*, played by the glorious Emma Thompson: "When you don't want me, but need me, then I will stay. When you want me, but no longer need me, then I will go."

Another coincidence, Charlie? I couldn't help but laugh all the way home.

AFTERWORD

Shikoku now gone, still I walk the *hachi jū hachi*.
One step.
Here rather than there.
—*Journal entry*

As I gazed into the pond at Ryōzenji, it was suddenly clear that the journey never ends, even though I had reached the destination. The cycle would perpetuate. As I turned and walked away from Ryōzenji, heading to the airport and then home, I knew, of course, that life behind the temple gates would continue without me, just as my life also would proceed without the 88 temples of Shikoku.

Waiting to board, I wrote this in my journal:

Translating the lessons from East to West,
country to town,
silence to noise.
Can it be done?
It must.

Translating the lessons from East to West,
country to town,
silence to noise.
Can it be done?
Little by little.
One step.

As euphoric as I was from what I had learnt, the work was just beginning again. What use are life-affirming lessons if not shared? What is the point of a newly opened heart and compassionate attitude if they fail to lighten the life of another? If one is not prepared to teach the art of "Universe Requesting" and guide others to manifest their personal bounties, then what is left? A lonely human hoarding memories and experience.

I have always wondered at the cave-dwelling ascetic. Tucked away high in a mountain cave, this spiritual student works as hard looking for understanding as an athlete does for Olympic gold. It's no picnic, I am certain of that, but I cannot help wondering if it is a little disingenuous. Without the challenges of the urban treadmill, is mountaintop contentment as much of an illusion as happiness is down amidst the busy foothills? Exercise is effortless on those days when you have plenty of energy; try doing it when you are tired and sore. It is easy to be pleasant to strangers when the sun is shining and all is well, yet try it when your head hurts and an unexpected utility bill drops through the letterbox. No strain is needed to calm yourself when sitting on a beach looking out over crystal blue waters; but can you keep the same level of well-being after a family argument?

I completed the 88 temple pilgrimage in 2007. It has taken this long for me to fulfil my duties of sharing what I had learnt because, in truth, I wasn't sure how. Initially, during my martial arts teaching, some of what I learnt has been paid forward albeit inadvertently, I hope. Now, with the passage of time, I have integrated the lessons of the 88 more comprehensively into my daily life. With everyday use of them, down from the mountain so to speak, my confidence in their value has burgeoned enough for me to feel secure sharing them. It was important for this to happen. As a teacher I have vowed never to teach something I have not fully understood through direct experience. The paper tigers that proliferate martial arts frustrate me.

Ninety percent of my students are children. I use the martial arts as a vehicle to teach schoolchildren self-confidence, a massive responsibility indeed. However, the confidence they attain is not won from a newly learnt set of self-defence techniques. It is born from something much more important, lasting, and meaningful, beyond the fearful confines of preparing for a bully who may not ever strike. Their confidence grows from what we in our school call "small wins": through the attainment and celebration of progressive challenges, our students begin to realise that success is not only possible but also likely with appropriate levels of work, focus, effort, and determination. In pilgrimage terminology this is the lesson of "one step". The other lessons of the 88 also began to organise themselves into pedagogic material, and I share them with confidence within the context of martial arts with all my students.

Naturally, a teacher is limited by the hours in a day, space in a room, and geography. I became acutely aware that a wider audience was missing out on the lessons of the 88, whether martial arts enthusiasts or not. So I decided to write this book and host workshops on the material. This book is for you from me; not because I am an authority on these matters and my voice counts more than yours, but because it is all that I have, and you deserve to know what the 88 has to share. Ultimately I recommend that you put this book down, book a flight, and walk the 88 yourself, really I do, but until then, please enjoy this.

These are the nine lessons from the 88:

1. Make a decision to begin.
2. Break down goals into small, achievable parts.
3. Learn what you need to learn to complete your goal.
4. Practice mindfulness meditation – Learn to be calm.
5. Universe Requesting – Ask for what you want.
6. Let go and relax.
7. Embrace the journey, the ups and the downs.
8. Don't forget kindness and love.
9. Trust that you have what it takes to be spectacular.

I believe sharing what we learn is only one half of being human. We must also continue to evolve and guard against becoming the "expert", the one who no longer needs to learn. This mistake is prevalent and abounds within the martial arts. For many, the black belt is a lifetime dream and goal. Students may spend years striving for this coveted prize, and quite correctly, they should enjoy it. But not too much! I cannot count the number of black belts who no longer push themselves as they once did when brown belts. It is sad to see.

I am not spouting from on high, with a voice of ego protesting my greatness. I am passing on the insight that was gifted to me as I looked into the koi pond back at Ryōzenji: that the journey never ends. Thankfully. If we stop evolving, striving, dreaming, experimenting, playing, and reinventing ourselves we are wasting a most precious gift: our lives. It is easy for us to take the foot off the pedal of our precious human birth; it tempts me no less than it does you. If you choose to stay like this, so be it; who am I to judge? But it seems a waste.

Ten years on I feel that my time to evolve has come again. My cycle continues to perpetuate, as do all of ours. I will teach and share what I have learnt and then return to the 88, to walk it all again. I wonder if it will be different this time around.

GLOSSARY OF TERMS

Bangai　番外 Other temples that are part of the history of the pilgrimage but not included in the 88 main sites.

Bodhisattva A Sanskrit term for anyone who, motivated by compassion, has the desire to attain Buddhahood for the benefit of all sentient beings.

Bonsai ぼなさい The Japanese art of cultivating miniature and dwarfed trees and shrubs.

Brahmin In Hinduism, the caste of priests, teachers, and protectors of sacred learning.

Buddha nature The name, in Buddhism, for the fundamental quality of all beings.

"Dark Night of the Soul" A poem by sixteenth-century Spanish poet and Roman Catholic mystic Saint John of the Cross.

Devas In Hinduism, the term for deities.

Dōgyō ninin　どお
ぎょおににん
A Japanese phrase that means "same practice, two people". It relates to the belief that Kōbō Daishi walks, in spirit, alongside pilgrims while on the 88.

Dōjō　どじょお
The Japanese name for a training hall commonly used for martial arts; literally translates as "hall of enlightenment".

Dōmo arigatō
gozaimasu　度も有
賀とございます
Japanese phrase for "Thank you very much".

Enkōji　えんこじ
Temple 39.

Fudō Myō-ō
ふどみょお
Japanese deity (wrathful).

Fujidera ふじでら
Temple 11.

Gaijin 外人
The Japanese word for "foreigner".

Gambatte kudasai
頑張っている
Japanese phrase meaning "Please take care". Often said to travellers and pilgrims walking the 88.

Hachi jū
hachi　八十八
Japanese for the number '88' (as in the 88 Temple pilgrimage).

Haiku　はいく
Short form Japanese poetry.

Hajime
はじめた
Japanese for 'begin'.

Hannya Shingyō 半やしんぎょお	The "Heart Sutra", one of the core prayers of Japanese Buddhism.
Hotsumisakiji ほつ みさきじ	Temple 24.
Henro 遍路	The Japanese word for "pilgrim".
Henro michi 遍路みち	The Japanese term for "the pilgrim's road".
Hiragana ひりがな	One of the three basic components of the Japanese writing system.
Ikebana 生け花	The Japanese art of flower arranging.
Ikimashou いき ましょう	Japanese phrase for "Let's go".
Jizō Bosatsu じぞ おぼさつ	Mythical Buddhist characters tasked with the job of saving people.
Jōrakuji じょ おらくじ	Temple 14.
Jūdō 柔道	The Japanese martial art of throwing and grappling.
Kanji かんじ	One of the three basic components of the Japanese writing system. Originally formulated in ancient China.

Karate 空手道 The Japanese martial art of punching, kicking and blocking.

Katakana カタカナ One of the three basic components of the Japanese writing system designed to describe foreign and imported words.

Katana 刀鍛冶 The famous Japanese long sword with a curved blade.

Keisaku けいさく Flat wooden paddle used to wake up, by striking, drowsy meditators while practising Zen Buddhist meditation.

Kōbō Daishi こおぼお Eighth Patriarch of *Shingon* Buddhism and creator of the 88 temple pilgrimage.

Kūkai くかい The Commonly used name for Kōbō Daishi.

Kyōhon きょおほn A book of Japanese Buddhist prayers.

Kyukeisho 休憩所 Japanese term for "rest area"".

Lao Tzu Ancient Chinese writer, philosopher and religious figure.

Maegamiji まえがみじ Temple 64.

Maslow's hierarchy of needs A theory in psychology proposed by Abraham Maslow regarding the needs of humans.

Mattō-san マットさ n	Japanese for "Mr Matt".
Myō-ō　明日	Gods said to be messengers of the Nyorai.
Nagaoji ながおじ	Temple 87.
Natsumikan 夏みかん	Type of Japanese citrus fruit.
Nirvana	A Sanskrit term typically associated with Buddhism to describe a perfect state of peace, happiness, and enlightenment.
Nyorai 如来	Enlightened beings.
Ohaiyō gozaimasu お肺よご ざいます	Japanese for "Good morning".
Ōkuboji おくぼじ	Temple 88.
Okimono 置物	Japanese term meaning "ornament for display".
Onaka ga akimashita お腹があ きました	Japanese phrase for "I am hungry"; literally translates as "stomach is empty".
Onsen 温泉	Japanese for 'hot spring'.

Prefecture	The name used for an administrative jurisdiction in Japan, much like *county* in the UK.
Reiki	A Japanese alternative treatment therapy said to rebalance subtle energies to activate the body's natural healing process.
Ryōkan 旅館	A type of traditional Japanese Inn.
Ryōzenji りょおぜんじ	Temple 1.
Salaryman サラリーマン	Japanese term for a 9-to-5 corporate office worker.
Samsara	A Sanskrit term typically associated with Buddhism to describe the endless cycle of life, death, and rebirth.
-san さん	Japanese honorific title when addressing or talking about others.
Shakyō 写経	The copying of sutra as a meditative practice.
Shiatsu　しあつ	A Japanese alternative treatment therapy said to rebalance subtle energies to activate the body's natural healing process - it is more hands on and dynamic than reiki.
Shidoji しどじ	Temple 86.

Shihan 市販	The Japanese title for "Master instructor".
Shikoku しこく	The Japanese island home to the 88-temple pilgrimage.
Shinto しんと	Indigenous religion of Japan.
Shodo 書道	The Japanese art of calligraphy.
Shōsanji しょさんじ	Temple 12.
Shunryu Suzuki 旬リュすずき	The author, monk, and teacher who popularised Zen Buddhism in the United States.
Sumi-e すみえ	The Japanese art of black ink painting.
Tenugui 手ぬぐい	Thin Japanese hand towel made of cotton.
Tokonama 床の間	A built-in recessed space found in a Japanese style reception room used to display spiritual or artistic ornaments.
Tsūyadō つやど	Huts or small makeshift facilities to serve as shelter for pilgrims on the 88.
Watashi wa Henro desu 私輪遍路です	Japanese phrase for "I am a pilgrim".
Yakuōji やくおじ	Temple 23.

Yakushi Nyorai 薬師如来	Buddha of healing.
Yin and Yang	A symbol, originating in China, now used widely in martial arts, traditional Chinese medicine and religion. Depicts context, contrast, and continuation.
Zen ぜん	A school of Buddhism.
*Zend*ō　全道	A hall where Zen Buddhists practise meditation.

SUGGESTED READING

Gallwey, Timothy W., *The Inner Game of Tennis: The ultimate guide to the mental side of peak performance:* Pan, Main Market ed. Edition, 18 Jun. 2015

Murray, W. H., *The Scottish Himalayan Expedition:* Dent, 1951

Nichtern, Ethan, *The Road Home: Buddhism for the 21st century:* Rider, 23 April 2015

Inoue, Enson, *Live as a Man. Die as a Man. Become a Man.: Volume 1 (The Way of the Modern Day Samurai):* CreateSpace Independent Publishing Platform; Volume 1 edition, 28 May 2014

Rinpoche, Sogyal, *The Tibetan Book of Living and Dying:* Rider, Reprint edition 1996

Burns, Robert, *Robert Burns, the Complete Poetical Works:* Alloway Publishing Ltd; Bi-centenary Ed Revised edition, 16 Dec. 1993

St. John of the Cross, *Dark Night of the Soul:* Dover, Thrift Editions

Moore, Thomas, *Dark Nights of the Soul: A guide to finding your way through life's ordeals:* Piatkus, 7 Jun. 2012

Walsch, Neale Donald, *Conversations with God, Book 1: An Uncommon Dialogue:* Hodder and Stoughton; New Ed edition, 6 Feb. 1997

ACKNOWLEDGEMENTS

I could not have done this alone. God knows, there would be one heck of a mess if it were left to me. So I have many people to thank. But there is a problem: I will undoubtedly forget someone. I know it will happen, no matter how long I sit here trying to think of everyone. If you know me, you know what I'm like. You know that I'm sorry, that I'm grateful, but I'm also forgetful.

Rarely do people who matter receive enough of the credit they deserve, and in my opinion not enough readers pay attention to the acknowledgements either. So I will be quizzing you at the end. I'll know who didn't do their homework!

First, a family is pivotal, despite the ups and downs: Mum and Dad; my brother, Nick; my wife, Sheri; and genius offspring, Sunni and India. I would apologise for all that you have had to put up with by being so close to me, but there is not enough ink in the world ....

These people helped shape my martial arts: Kris Wilder, Lee Hasdell, Enson Inoue, Roger Gracie, FB and the David Brothers, Morio Higaonna, John Ding, Masaji Taira, Geoff Thompson, Peter Consterdine, and Patrick McCarthy. The best of these teachers? Every student I have ever had. Your work and efforts have allowed me to find a way that is my own. Thank you.

Dudley Georgeson, Keith Reynolds, and Adrian Rattenbury started me off on the journey of teaching. I am forever grateful. Things you have said still stay at the front of my mind, even after all these years.

Sogyal Rinpoche, first your book and then your teachings brought meditation and Buddhism into my life. I am richer for it in every way. "Thank you" doesn't seem enough. Ethan Nichtern, your modern version has been instrumental to me.

The Ridolfis, Suzanne and Ray, taught me so much more than just shiatsu; lessons, planted years ago, are still blossoming today.

Mike Lax, Jim Foxhall, Rami Ajami and Will Henshaw, Drew Sullivan, Alessandro Saba, Gareth Baxendale, xiaobaosg, and Pam Grout have all impacted the *Hardest Path* projects. Thank you all. You are important pieces of this great puzzle.

Dan Frost, Jeremy Clark, Pieter and Nicky Jooste, and Lewis Jones – you know your value to JK and more importantly to me, as friends.

In the world of writing, the work of the maestro, Paulo Coelho, showed me that you could write introspectively without having to make it weird. More than anything, I hope I've done that for you. Callum Medcraft and Mike Summers allowed me to share my thoughts and words with the world by letting me loose on *Jiu Jitsu Style* magazine and *Podium* respectively. Thank you, guys. Adam Scofield, Frances Cutts, Kris Wilder, Amanda Cooper, Sheri Jardine, and Robbie Colon; the value of your feedback is immeasurable: this is *our* book. Except the profits. They're mine. Hands off.

I believe that the Universe is on our side and that we are designed to win. With that in mind, I thank it.

OK, that's it for the thanks, with forgetful omissions, and now time for the quiz: I didn't thank Jane Dun Srini directly, nor did I forget this exotic-sounding lovely. She is, in fact, an anagram of someone I did thank. Who is it? (Just for fun, no prizes, but it would be fun if you post the answer on my FB page: https://www.facebook.com/hardestpath/)

YOU MAY ALSO LIKE THESE

I suspect that there is a ninja spy hanging upside somewhere in my house. Why this paranoia? Because every time I buy anything online, someone emails, calls, or messages to suggest that they could offer something similar that I may like to purchase further.

So I feel I should jump on this bandwagon, in fear of my son accusing me of not "getting with the times".

Joking aside, I mention these future projects because I believe in them, and I hope they may be of service to you in some small way.

LIVING THE HARDEST PATH
WORKSHOPS IN THE NINE LESSONS OF THE **88**

First and foremost I am a teacher, and I am happy to share with you the nine lessons of the 88.

My wish is that you may take the information from these workshops and apply them successfully to your lives.

If you would like to contact us about arranging a school assembly, workshops, courses, team training, or talks, please contact us at this email address: courses@thehardestpath.com

HAIKU OF A *HENRO*

I documented my pilgrimage by both video and written journal.

Haiku of a *Henro* (the Japanese word for pilgrim) is the collection of thoughts, insights, and wisdom that were gifted to me while on pilgrimage.

I wrote them down as they came to me, and I feel, both then and now, that I was the recipient rather than the creator of them. They are unedited, pure, and in the order that I received them.

These will be released late 2016 or early 2017. Keep your eyes on the hardest path website to order your copy: www.thehardestpath.com

CONTACT US

I would love to connect with you. If you would like to say hi, share your thoughts on the book, ask anything about the pilgrimage, or generally "chew the fat" about these sorts of things, please visit our Facebook page: https://www.facebook.com/hardestpath/

A NOTE ABOUT THE AUTHOR

Matt Jardine is an author, writer, athlete, and teacher.

He is the founder of Jardine Karate and has helped thousands of students discover their personal potential through his specially designed martial arts programmes. He teaches in schools throughout London and at his Surrey venues.

Matt writes for *Jiu Jitsu Style* magazine, Europe's largest Brazilian jiu-jitsu magazine, and is the author of Mo and Lucy-choices, a top ten–rated PHSE resource for school students.

He has practised meditation and other Eastern arts for over twenty-five years and now lives in London with his wife and Jack Russell. He has two grown-up children.

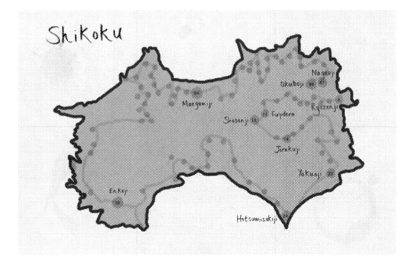

Printed in the United States
By Bookmasters